T0182691

TOUGH RUGGED BASTARDS

A MEMOIR OF A LIFE IN MARINE SPECIAL OPERATIONS

JOHN A. DAILEY

A KNOX PRESS BOOK
An Imprint of Permuted Press
ISBN: 978-1-63758-735-5
ISBN (eBook): 978-1-63758-736-2

Tough Rugged Bastards:
A Memoir of a Life in Marine Special Operations
© 2024 by John A. Dailey
All Rights Reserved

Cover art by Conroy Accord

This is a work of nonfiction. All people, locations, events, and situations are portrayed to the best of the author's memory, but where security may be a concern, first names only are used.

No part of this book may be reproduced, stored in a retrieval system, or transmitted by any means without the written permission of the author and publisher.

Permuted Press, LLC
New York • Nashville
permutedpress.com

Published in the United States of America
1 2 3 4 5 6 7 8 9 10

Dedicated to the men of Detachment One,
and to all Recon Marines, Raiders, and Scout Snipers
past, present, and future:

Never above you
Never below you
Always beside you

TABLE OF CONTENTS

INTRODUCTION

God is not on the side of the big battalions,
but on the side of those who shoot best.
—Voltaire

Najaf, Iraq—August 2004

You were not the first man I'd killed, but you're the one I think of most often. The other times it was dark, chaotic. We called it "the fog of war." I was on a mountainside, or roadside, or in a building, and bullets were going both ways. Killing was often a shared responsibility. Maybe my bullets found the other men, or maybe someone else's did. You were different; your face filled my rifle scope. My shot split the morning silence. There was no doubt about you.

This isn't an apology, just an explanation. And I guess it's a way for me to look back and try and make sense of it all. I have never doubted that if things had gone the other way, you would've pulled the trigger. I'd be dead and you'd be sitting somewhere, maybe thinking of me— maybe not. Instead, I carry the weight of you and the others. You're not as heavy as you once were, but the weight will never vanish completely. I wouldn't want it to.

I've wondered how you wound up there that day. Was it chance? It's funny how a million little things could have made a difference. If you had been a street over, or if I had picked another building, I would never have seen you. But then again sometimes I feel my whole life had been leading me there, to *that* rooftop *that* morning: a twisted line that stretched back thirty-five years from that rooftop in Najaf, Iraq to a distant past in the little village of Hillsboro, Virginia. Given the countless thousands of decisions and choices and nudges and interventions it took to bring us together, maybe we were exactly where we were supposed to be.

In combat, a lot of guys write death letters to a parent or wife or child. Sealed and entrusted to a friend—only to be delivered in the event of their death. I never wrote one. I told everyone I thought they were bad luck, but truthfully, I didn't know what to write. I had no idea how to try to sum up the things I ought to say to the people I loved, my deathbed thoughts, when death wasn't imminent. I chose, selfishly perhaps, to believe in my own immortality.

I've wondered if you wrote a letter—and if it was ever delivered.

But now that twisted line has stretched almost twenty years, from that morning into a future that I had no way of seeing then; nearly seven thousand sunrises and sunsets. I've crested the half-century mark and find myself looking back at that time with a mixture of awe and incredulity, amazed that I have made it this far, and honored that I once had the chance to stand among the men I called teammates and friends.

I felt so lucky to be one of the few Colonel Coates picked to serve in Detachment One and thrilled to be chosen to lead a team. But I was also baffled as to why. Afraid that at any moment he would realize he made a mistake, that I didn't belong, and even more afraid that I would do something to prove it. Of course, then I thought I was the only one who felt that way. Undeserving of the opportunity, unready for the responsibility. And so, I did what I had learned to do: bury my self-doubt in bravado, and hide behind the same mask of self-assuredness we all wore. But now I see that is what pushed us so hard. The need to be worthy of the trust placed in us, the obligation to earn our place on the team every day, and the knowledge that the future of Marine special operations rested on our shoulders.

CHAPTER 1

WE'RE OFF TO SEE
THE ELEPHANT

So, let me go and leave your safety behind me;
Go to the spaces of hazard where
nothing shall bind me;
Go till the word is War—and then you will find me.
—Robert William Service

A note about names: Many of the Marines I served with, and will mention, are still involved in sensitive work on behalf of the nation. For this reason, I use only first names, or nicknames for the Marines in the teams I worked with. I use ranks and full names of the commanders that I worked for.

The table at Kitty O'Shea's pub was covered in empty and half-empty beer pitchers. That they were pitchers of Victoria Bitter provided the reminder that we were on Mitchell Street in Darwin, Australia, and not some other Irish pub on some other country's coast. Around us, other Marines drank, and rugby-shirted Aussies hollered at the football highlights playing on TVs mounted above the bar.

Nights on Mitchell Street are crazy any time ships are in. And since the arrival of the Fifteenth Marine Expeditionary Unit (Special Operations Capable), or MEU SOC, brought 2,500 Marines and an equal number of sailors, all of whom had been training in the Northern

Territory for the past week, this night was destined to turn wild quickly. The best bet was to find a small, out-of-the-way pub and tuck into a beer.

I was the platoon sergeant for a thirty-man Force Reconnaissance platoon. It was my job to take care of the training, welfare, and tactical employment of the platoon. I answered to the platoon commander, Captain Phil Treglia. Our mission as the Force Reconnaissance element of the Fifteenth MEU was to conduct amphibious reconnaissance, deep ground reconnaissance, surveillance, battlespace-shaping, and limited-scale raids. We were the primary reason that the MEU was designated SOC—Special Operations Capable.

We had spent the past week training with Australian snipers and sleeping in hammocks strung between trees near the range complex. Earlier in the afternoon we had packed up, returned to the USS *Peleliu*, and cleaned up for a night on the town. I was out with my three team leaders, Willy, Smitty, and Jack. We were all married and content to suck down beers while the young Marines were off searching for the legendary Australian ladies of questionable morals.

On the month-long transit of the Pacific Ocean, we had volunteered our services to help the MEU helicopter pilots complete one of their qualifications, called S.P.I.E. rigging (Special Patrol Insertion/ Extraction). This involved us treading water in the middle of the ocean as they hovered overhead and tossed out a thick rope. One end of the line was connected securely to the aircraft. On the other end, a series of metal loops were woven into the rope. As the helicopter flew over, the crew chief kicked the coiled rope through the opening in the floor called the "hellhole." When the line landed in the water we swam to it, clipped our harness in, and once set, were lifted out of the water to fly in a circle before being dunked back into the ocean to unclip and wait for the next pilot's turn.

This is considerably less fun than you might imagine it to be, but it breaks up the monotony of ship life, which largely consists of sleeping, eating, reading books, and working out inside of a hot metal box surrounded by a thousand of your closest, sweaty friends.

But now we were reaping the reward. In appreciation for our assistance, a group of the pilots, who were bellied up to the bar, kept our table covered in pitchers of beer. There is a saying in the Marine Corps that fairy tales begin with "Once upon a time," but sea stories start with "No shit, there I was." It was turning into that kind of night. And so, we drank and rehashed stories that grew in scope with each telling.

Willy was recounting an episode from a training deployment we had completed some months earlier, a practice High Altitude–High Opening parachute infiltration on a desert base in China Lake, California. On the last night of our trip, we convinced the staff of the base's enlisted club to let us stay after closing time. After a hard night of drinking, Willy and I were watching the sunrise through the window when he heard a ruckus coming from the kitchen. We walked in to find Smitty dressed in a chef's cap, apron, and little else, cooking an obscenely large quantity of frozen hash brown patties on the club's enormous flattop griddle. That was about the time that a member of the base's civilian guard force entered and bellowed, "If I have to tell you again to leave, you ain't going to the barracks, you're going to jail!" While we all been there and had heard the story repeatedly, Willy's imitation of the guard always brought a fit of laughter.

We were still laughing when the bartender roared, "Oy, mates!" and dug for the remote to push up the TV's volume. It was 10:32 p.m. for us; 9:02 a.m. Eastern Standard Time.

It was hard to recognize what I was seeing—a tall building shot from an unsteady camera, a plume of smoke. An accident of some kind. And then the camera panned out to a sister building and another airplane that set us all on a collision course.

Almost immediately the Marines in uniform designated as shore patrol began running down the length of Mitchell Street, holding radios to their ears, poking heads in the bar doors and shouting, "We've been attacked! Back to the ships, now!" Around us, tables emptied as Marines rushed out.

We all stood, stunned. And then Willy, who I could always count on for clarity in crisis, looked around and said, "This is the last night out we're going to have for a long while."

I nodded and looked at the pitchers. "Shame to let them go to waste."

We sat back down and stared at the TVs, pouring beer down our throats, until we had cleared the table and the bartender said, "Ya gotta go. You're the only Yanks left in town."

***

September 11, 2021—This morning I went for a walk on the sandy trails running through Hammocks Beach State Park near my eastern North Carolina home. It was still humid for September; I wore shorts and a T-shirt that was soon pasted to my back. The three interconnected trails are marked red, white, and blue. This early in the morning I had them to myself. I turned left at the first juncture, then right, and left again. I walked for hours, lost in a labyrinth of long-leaf pine and thought. But each trail eventually led back to the starting point, and all roads led to the home I needed to get back to, and to the seat at my computer that I had been avoiding for too long.

I've spent twenty years trying to piece together the patchwork of thoughts and memories, lessons and lamentations. Twenty years trying to make sense of it. Twenty years to realize that I'm not ever likely to, but I can still see the value in the trying. Trying to live by the maxim from Marcus Aurelius that I first read almost twenty years ago. "Think of the life you have lived until now as over and, as a dead man, see what's left as a bonus and live it according to Nature. Love the hand that fate deals you and play it as your own, for what could be more fitting?" I look back to a time when I felt I knew everything and had so much to offer.

Now, I realize I still have much to learn, and nothing to offer but words, but I am grateful for the hand I get to play and hope to play it well.

***

I cannot recall with any clarity a time before I knew I wanted to be a Marine, but I do remember the day I decided.

It was the summer of 1976. I was nearly seven years old. Like towns across the South, Purcellville, Virginia held a combination Fourth of July parade, covered-dish dinner, and bluegrass jamboree. That year's festivities took on a fevered pitch as it was the bicentennial of our nation's birth. The Vietnam War was over, and the nation was looking to heal itself. I was, of course, oblivious to all of this. The highlight for me had been to receive a red, white, and blue plastic change purse bearing the name of the local savings and loan from a stilt-wearing Uncle Sam.

Then I looked up and saw him, walking through the crowd: a US Marine in his dress-blue uniform. I still see him now through the eyes of a six-year-old. A grizzled, chisel-jawed sergeant with numerous combat tours under his belt, and a deep, red scar zigzagging the length of his face to disappear under his high, dress-blue collar. I imagined it to be a dying gift from Viet Cong sapper. His immaculate, dark-blue uniform jacket bore row upon row of ribbons. A wide, blood-red stripe ran down the seam of his pants' legs, and spit-shined shoes reflected the hot July sun.

It is far more likely that he was an eighteen-year-old private, fresh out of boot camp, and still sporting adolescent acne. But this is one of many memories whose accuracy is far less important than the weight it carries. I knew from that moment that I would wear that uniform. I tugged on my dad's pant leg and asked, "What is that man?"

"That's a Marine," said my dad, who had served in the navy. "We called them jarheads."

In my memory, he followed that statement with, "They're some tough bastards."

I suspect that I added that comment to the conversation somewhere along the way. Bastard was not a word Dad usually threw around to his six-year-old son. He does not recall the exchange or even the event, but I am unable to call up the memory any differently.

The Marine faded back into the crowd never to be seen again. The seed, however, had been planted. I went through phases, of course, where I imagined other careers. For a brief period, I thought about being president. I wanted to play shortstop for the Baltimore Orioles.

I flirted with long-haul truck driving. I liked the idea of a life on the road, and I was curious about the various vending machines located in truck-stop restrooms. But through it all, I held, somewhere in the back of my brain, a picture of myself in that uniform. And I think that from that moment forward I began to make choices that eventually would lead me to a career in the Marine Corps.

***

September 12, 2001 dawned, and we were back out to sea with headaches and questions. Somehow, we managed to collect up all the drunken Marines and sailors and get them on board before weighing anchors and casting off in the dark. News about the attacks was sporadic. Computer access already was limited, and the lines for the several ship-to-shore phones stretched down narrow passageways. I wrote letters and posted them not knowing when they would be received. Occasional updates arrived via satellite news, and the rumor mill churned with everyone hearing from some "very reliable source" where we were headed and what we were destined for.

My wife, Tracy, and children, Garrett (seven) and Kallie (five), were at home on base in Camp Pendleton, California. I trusted that they were safe and would be taken care of, but I knew that Tracy understood, as we did, that I was going to war. So I waited in line for the chance to punch in the number on my phone card and assure her that everything would be all right. When I got through, as usual I downplayed any possibility of danger, and as usual she tried to stay upbeat, passing the phone to the kids, who wanted to tell me about their new classes. I wanted to listen, but the line of men growing down the passageway forced me to cut them off with, "You can tell me the rest later. I love you. Can you put Mom back on?"

There is nothing like impending conflict to liven up the drudgery of shipboard life. Our days were now a flurry of preparations, though we were not completely sure what we were preparing for. Before we left the States, I requested permission to paint our forest-green Mercedes-Benz G-Wagons to match desert terrain. I was told that if and when we went to war, we could. I took our situation as a reasonable affirmation of permission and set a team to playing with the color palette of paints available on a navy ship. They were able to arrive at a tannish hue we felt would blend in with desert sand, and so in the well deck of the ship, armed with rollers and brushes, the boys painted away. Once the paint dried and met the sunlight, we realized that the color was considerably more pink than tan. I took some solace in the fact that in the 1960s, after significant testing, the British Special Air Service determined that pink was a highly effective desert camouflage, especially at dawn and dusk. They painted their Land Rovers a bright shade that earned the vehicles the nickname "pinkies."

We were outfitted with desert uniforms, but our packs and load-bearing equipment were also woodland camouflage. Somehow, we procured cases of tan spray paint and braved the fumes and the ire of navy chiefs at the overspray, and we toned down our equipment.

On October 7, offensive combat operations officially began. This consisted primarily of air and missile strikes against known Taliban targets. Army Special Forces teams were already in place operating with the Northern Alliance. On that day, my platoon was sent in to establish security at Pasni Airport, a small airfield on the Pakistani coast. Once secure, men and material were brought ashore by helicopter and landing craft to stage and await the five-hundred-mile C-130 flight to Jacobabad, Pakistan, which would become the initial Search and Rescue (SAR) airfield and staging base for special operations in Afghanistan.

A week or so later, we returned to the ship sitting off the coast in the North Arabian Sea, to find that we had been selected by the MEU commander, Colonel Thomas Waldhauser, to fly into Afghanistan in advance of the landing force to observe and report on a small desert airfield that had been designated "Camp Rhino." While planning for the mission, we determined that US Special Operations Command (USSOCOM) helicopters would be best-suited to make the flight and requested their support for insertion.

As we continued to plan, at some level above us the decision was made that it would be the Navy SEALs, not Force Recon, who inserted to conduct the initial reconnaissance. I was (I think understandably) furious that the MEU's first boots on the ground and eyes on Camp Rhino would be SEAL boots and SEAL eyes. This was the first time I observed first-hand the power and reach of USSOCOM.

Ultimately, there was no activity for the SEALs to observe. The airfield was abandoned, a fact that did little to assuage the sting of being sidelined. We made our way to Camp Rhino on November 25, and almost immediately sent out Smitty's team on a vehicle patrol to conduct reconnaissance of the dirt roads and trails that crisscrossed the area, and to implant seismic intrusion sensors that allowed us to monitor movement along the roadways leading toward Rhino.

I only recently learned that what we called Camp Rhino had been a hunting camp for wealthy Afghan falconers. The compound was surrounded by a ten-foot, earth-colored wall, as much to keep out the blowing sand of the Registan Desert as to prevent intruders. Guard towers rose from the four corners of the compound to thirty feet, and from their vantage point the talcum-powder sand stretched out flat and cratered, like the surface of a sandy moon. A drought several years prior had led the desert's nomadic occupants to seek shelter elsewhere. When the winds picked up, the desert itself would rise and race toward Rhino in a hulking cloud that ate the sun and sandblasted anything in its path. Outside of the walls, a dirt airstrip was barely discernable from the desert that fought daily to reclaim it. It was a Sisyphean effort by the Marine engineers and Navy Seabee teams to keep the surface clear and stable for the C-130 and C-17 flights that poured in each night, packed with all the supplies needed to sustain a well-armed, mid-sized town in a frozen, waterless hell.

CHAPTER 2

IT PAYS TO BE A WINNER

*Through every generation of the human race
there has been a constant war, a war with
fear. Those who have the courage to conquer
it are made free and those who are conquered
by it are made to suffer until they have the
courage to defeat it, or death takes them.*

—Alexander the Great

After a few days of getting settled in, Captain Treglia and I were summoned to the small, sand-colored, concrete building that served as the MEU operations center. Our MEU and a sister East Coast MEU were now assigned to a new headquarters dubbed Task Force Fifty-Eight, commanded by Brigadier General James Mattis (who would later be known by the world as "Mad Dog"). We were directed to prepare for an overland vehicle route reconnaissance from Rhino to a point just outside of Kandahar, about one hundred miles away. By traveling across the open desert, we hoped to reach our destination undetected.

We took off at night, our vehicles led by a Marine single file, like a string of goats, through the perimeter of fighting holes that circled the airfield, and the labyrinth of razor wire meant to slow any attackers. Once beyond friendly lines, our vehicles spread out into an inverted V formation, like a flock of geese. The lead vehicle followed a compass azimuth north, deviating as the desert terrain dictated. The formation expanded when possible and contracted when necessary. As we picked our way through wadi and ditch, we stopped frequently to dismount a guide to lead the vehicles. The moon was waning, gibbous but still nearly full—massive and high in the sky, so that when we hit the large, flat stretches and came up to speed, we flew across the desert, an unauthorized American flag flying from a radio antenna. We had been directed not to fly the American flag because we did not want to be seen as invaders, but it was night and it looked really cool. The desert air was shockingly cold. The abundance and brilliance of stars on the coal-black sky in a desert devoid of light pollution made it hard to gaze skyward without imagining a divine hand, and wondering if its owner was watching and what it had in store for us.

Before sunup, we located a dip in the terrain and established a security perimeter we called a laager site. We followed the acronym S.A.F.E. to establish our priorities of work: Security, Automatic Weapons, Fields of Fire, and Entrenching. I sent several men with their weapons to provide security, while some dismounted our machine guns, carried them to the high ground, and established positions to scan the featureless desert. Others set up comm; still others stretched camouflage nets over poles shoved into the sand to hide our vehicles and provided a scant amount of shade. Finally, we cleaned weapons before eating and at last catching a little sleep.

As dusk fell, we reversed the process and set out again, arriving at the link-up location in the middle of the night. Once again, we established security and waited for the remainder of the task force to catch up. When they arrived, we added to our numbers: light armored vehicles, heavy-machine-gun and rocket-wielding armored HMMWVs (Humvees), and a headquarters staff who would be orchestrating our actions. Fuel problems and the fine desert sand sidelined several vehicles, and a portion of the force under the command of Captain Treglia had to remain behind, leaving me in charge of the two remaining teams led by Jack and Matt.

General Mattis had tasked us with executing strikes against the Taliban on the roads and deserts outside of Kandahar. We harbored up during the day and went out at night conducting reconnaissance and looking for signs of Taliban activity, but everywhere we looked wound up empty. After a few days without contact, I was directed to establish a vehicle ambush on Highway One.

We departed the patrol base at dusk, leaving behind enough security to hold the position against attack. My guys moved out in advance, confirming the route, and locating a fording site to cross a Helmand River tributary.

At that time, Highway One ran from Kabul through Kandahar and Lashkar Gah, then eventually north to Herat. Later expansion would complete the loop through Mazar-i-Sharif back to Kabul. The roadway was built on top of a high berm, sloping away on either side to prevent the desert sand from taking over. To the north, flat desert began to give way to the Hindu Kush Himalayan region peaks that stretched skyward. The convoy paused at a point on the map indistinguishable from any other point, but invisible in the darkness; several thousand meters to our front lay the highway.

**Me and the boys the morning after our Highway One
gunfight in Afghanistan on 6–7 December 2001**

After confirming the plan, we left the rest of the task force behind and pushed forward with two vehicles from the combined anti-armor platoon. They unstrapped heavy rolls of concertina wire from the hoods of their vehicles. Concertina wire, or razor wire, comes in coils, like a three-foot-high child's Slinky, except with sharpened blades spaced along its length. It is often used on a unit's perimeter to slow or canalize attacking infantry, but it is also effective against vehicles. The Marines helped us stretch concertina wire tight across the road and stake it down; then they loaded up and drove off to cover our flanks, leaving us on the roadside.

I directed Matt to move his G-Wagon with a mounted heavy machine gun to a location where he would be able to provide firepower on the concertina obstacle if needed. I assumed that any Taliban would be leaving Kandahar, so I positioned my vehicle off the road in that direction. The idea was that as they passed us sitting below the berm, we would drive up behind them, boxing them between us and the obstacle.

I was worried about encountering civilians fleeing Kandahar. We had been told that anyone on the roads was declared hostile (which meant we could shoot without identification), but that wasn't an order I was willing to give. That was why we had been picked to do this. We were shooters; we were trained to shoot discriminately and hit what we aimed at. We needed to be smarter and better than everyone else.

There was a picture that floated in the back of my mind and haunted me. It was executing a perfectly laid ambush, and then approaching the bullet-torn vehicle to discover a family who died trying to flee from the evil we were there to stop.

I wouldn't be responsible for any of my men having to carry that burden, and I didn't think that I could. So, we would conduct the operation not as an ambush but as a vehicle assault, which we were trained to do. Once the vehicle was stopped, we would take up positions along the rear and left side of the vehicle using our weapon-mounted flashlights to blind and disorient the occupants. At the first sign of hostility, all bets were off and everyone in the vehicle would die.

We went through a few test runs, to make sure that our vehicle could easily scale the high berm. We walked through the plan and rehearsed contingencies, then took our positions to wait. Through a headset, I stayed in communication with the aircraft overhead, and the rest of the task force remained hidden behind dunes a half-mile away. After some time, we received word that a convoy of vehicles was leaving Kandahar and coming toward us. The aircraft reported that occasionally the lead vehicle, a pickup truck, would drive ahead to scout while the other, larger vehicles would pull off into the desert to wait.

The December air was frigid, and we were ill-equipped for it. My lower lip was cracked from the cold and perpetually oozing blood. We were wrapped in our Gore-Tex rain gear to fight the wind, and at that moment it was doing very little to keep the frozen air at bay. As we sat, I joked with Pope, our platoon parachute rigger in the driver's seat that while some people were bullet magnets, I was the opposite, a bullet repellent.

In boot camp, a drill instructor told us that we should expect to see combat in our four-year tour. It had now been fourteen years, and the closest I had come was observing a coup attempt from the rooftop of the American Embassy in Buenos Aires, Argentina.

I had requested embassy duty in 1989 for the excitement it promised. I was assigned initially to the American Embassy in Budapest, Hungary. It was a great experience. There I met Tracy—a Pittsburgh girl, fresh from receiving her teaching degree from Penn State, who was teaching at the American School in Budapest. After a year in Budapest, I was transferred to Buenos Aires, where I sat out the Gulf War, and I was ashamed and embarrassed about that. After my return, I found myself on the wrong deployment rotation for Somalia in 1992. So, like the Marines under my charge, I had not seen combat, and given my track record, I was having a hard time wrapping my head around the idea that it would happen tonight.

I listened to the chatter between the forward air controller and the aircraft as the vehicles drew closer. Again, the trail vehicles, which were described as large, troop-carrying transports, pulled off the road and let the lead vehicle push forward alone toward our position.

The radio crackled in my ear. It was the flank security team. "We've got visual on the lead vehicle. They're passing us now. An extended-cab truck. The back is packed with boxes and a few men."

"Solid copy. No visual on the other vehicles?"

"Negative."

I turned and passed a final update to Pope and the guys in the bed of the vehicle. "Get ready, do what we rehearsed. It's an easy day." There wasn't time for speeches or steeling words, but I knew they were prepared.

Now I could see the vehicle approaching in the moonlight. It drove without headlights in the mistaken belief that it could hide from our aircraft. As the truck passed us, I slapped Pope on the shoulder. "Go!"

He brought us up to speed and hit the berm. As we settled onto the road, I was staring into the faces of three men, bundled against the incredible cold. Through my night-vision goggles, I could see their expressions change from drowsy, frozen, and bored to incomprehension as to how we had suddenly appeared behind them. They were seated on boxes with their knees up against the raised tailgate of the truck. The men on either side were completely bundled, with only their beards poking out from the blankets that covered them and wrapped around the weapons they carried. The man in the center kept his AK-47 exposed, and with it his bare hands gripped the cold wood and metal. Through night vision, everything was green, but I could picture his hands—red, stinging, and callused.

They didn't have time to react. The driver may have seen the wire but couldn't stop, or perhaps thought he could drive through it.

I had never seen a vehicle run into properly laid concertina wire. The effect was almost instantaneous. The wire wrapped itself around the axles; the truck fought against it, but was pulled to a stop, the wire stretching until it ran down the length of the truck. Pope hit the brakes, coming to a stop ten feet from the men who were now fully awake with the reality of their situation settling in.

At this exact second, something happened. I didn't look at my watch to see how it was measured, but time slowed almost to a stop, for everyone but me. That is the only way to explain it that comes close to giving any sense of how I felt. It wasn't that I was moving or thinking faster, it was that everyone around me had slowed to a glacial pace, and my perspective shifted. It was as though I was ten feet tall, seeing everything with a god's-eye view.

I leap from the passenger-side door. Pope remains behind the wheel in case we need to move. Doc is in the bed of the vehicle, leaning over the roof with the squad automatic weapon, covering the truck. Jack, Dave, T.C., and Roman jump from the back and take up positions on either side of me.

I yell out in English, "Drop your weapons!" A command they can't understand and won't comply with. I am focused on the center man. He is older with streaks of gray and ice in his beard. He is fumbling to free himself from the blanket that keeps him from raising his weapon. His movements are so slow as to barely register.

While he struggles with his weapon, a great calm comes over me. My rifle is in my shoulder, his chest is centered underneath the red dot of my Aimpoint sight. My thumb flips the selector switch from safe to fire and my finger curls around the trigger. These are all actions I have practiced a hundred thousand times on the ranges of Camp Pendleton.

From my narrowed periphery, the muzzles of rifles on either side of me rise. The old man's AK is now free but rising comically slow. I can see the weapon even now. The stock is scarred, the metal almost white from cleaning with kerosene; wire wraps the front handguard. The thought runs through my head that I would bring that weapon back and mount it on a plaque in the First Force Recon Headquarters. Then I admonish myself for having ridiculous thoughts when a man is trying to shoot me.

I fire a controlled pair, two rounds to his chest from my M4 carbine. I expect him to fall, but he remains in place, wedged between his comrades and the boxes.

We are not wearing earplugs, but the sound of my shots is barely audible, pop, pop, like popcorn on the stove at home instead of the earsplitting crack that I associate with 5.56 rounds.

Muzzles flash in my peripheral vision, but I don't hear any shots except my own. I fire two rounds to each body, one to each head. Puffs of dirt blossom from the blankets with each torso shot. I don't stop to survey the damage. We are trained to fire a "box drill," a controlled pair to the chest of each target then up to the heads. The bodies absorb far more bullets than are needed to accomplish the task.

Truck doors scrape against the wire as the men inside the cab struggle to get out. A man on the left makes it but doesn't have the chance to raise his rifle. Our fire is disciplined and slow into the cab of the truck.

Then from the truck bed, a flicker of flame. Our tracer rounds ignited the cargo. In an instant, the bed is engulfed. I turn and motion to Pope to begin backing up the vehicle. I look over to Jack who is completing a head count, then signals that we are up, everyone is accounted for. As flame sweeps through the truck more men emerge from the cab like a flaming clown car, some on fire. We drop them with quick pairs and begin bounding backward away from the inferno.

Pope drives back down from the road onto the desert floor. We follow on foot, bounding away. Moving in two-man teams, so that there are always guns pointed at the truck that is now what firefighters would describe as "fully involved."

What remained of the Taliban truck on 7 December 2001.

When I turned my back on the truck, time returned to its normal speed and sound resumed its pitch. I could feel the warmth of the fire and hear the truck's sheet metal buckle and pop from the heat. The sickening smell of burnt hair and charred flesh, and an undertone of cooking meat, slapped me in the face.

I looked to where Matt's truck was parked. And punched the radio button on my chest. "Are y'all good?"

"Roger, we're up. Want me to come to you?"

"Hold what you got. Cover our withdraw until we're set."

"Roger."

We moved a hundred yards from the fire and formed a tight perimeter, taking a knee and facing outboard. Jack made a quick circuit and returned with an ACE report: Ammo, Casualties, and Equipment. No one had fired more than half of a mag, everyone was healthy, and everyone had all the gear they started with. The SOP (Standard Operating Procedure) was to get a count of the Enemy KIA and search them for information of intel value, but that would have to wait. I prepared to pass our status to the rest of the task force waiting at the ORP (Objective Rally Point).

Then, from the truck, the pop of bullets. How could anyone have survived that? We dropped forward into the prone position and looked for the shooter. I keyed the mike to tell Matt to light them up but stopped. From the bed of the flaming truck, I heard a whoosh and an RPG rocket launched. But instead of heading for us, it spiraled into the night sky and, because it had not been armed, landed harmlessly in the desert without detonating. Then we realized that the bed of the truck was full of ammunition cooking off in the flames. Crates of RPG rockets began to tumble like pinwheels into the night. We piled back into the vehicles and moved away.

I communicated with the forward air controller who was working the aircraft, dropping bombs on the remaining vehicles hiding in the desert, and requested that he have them drop a bomb on the flaming hulk in hope that it would destroy any sign that we had been there, and allow us to retain the element of surprise for the following night.

***

There is a euphoria that comes after a gunfight. Some of it comes from surviving, some from the knowledge that you acquitted yourself well. I felt immense pride in the way the guys performed, as if it validated my job as a leader, but I think a lot of it comes from the god-like feeling of control over life and death.

We linked back up with the remainder of the force and drove back to the patrol base, arriving at daybreak. I conducted a quick after-action review with the guys whose heads now were bobbing—the result of a long night, but even more as the price we paid for the flood of chemicals that coursed through our veins during the fight. When the danger subsides, the body tries to return to stasis. The rush of adrenaline and endorphins subsides and is replaced by a bone-deep weariness that demands sleep. I promised them we'd pick it up after we rested. I dug into my ruck for a large plastic flask full of dark rum that I had carried for just the right occasion and passed it around. It was just enough to warm the belly and cloud the mind, and the men bedded down for some much-needed and well-deserved sleep.

I sat wrapped in my sleeping bag and went back over the mission—what had gone well, what could have gone better—and made notes. I was fascinated by the time, sound, and vision distortions I experienced, and vowed to learn more about the phenomenon and how to control it.

The next morning, Pope found a bullet hole in the windshield post of his vehicle. We had been unaware of any return fire, but the enemy got off at least one shot.

The official estimates speculated that eighty to one hundred Taliban were killed that night. Ten had been crammed in the pickup, and the rest were spread between the trucks obliterated by aircraft in the desert. The next day, when we drove through on our way to Kandahar, the bodies had been removed, but the hulk of the truck sat stranded on the roadway. I told my driver to slow down just long enough to jump out and slap a New York Fire Department bumper sticker on the blackened metal.

Over the next several nights, we set up similar ambushes with no success. On the outskirts of Kandahar, we swapped out with the East Coast Twenty-Sixth MEU and returned to Camp Rhino.

While we had been running around southern Afghanistan, in the North, Army Special Forces teams and CIA officers were fighting alongside Afghan Northern Alliance fighters in the Battle of Qala-i-Jangi, after over four hundred fighters surrendered outside of Mazar-i-Sharif. Later, the prisoners revolted and the ensuing battle lasted six days. Former Marine and CIA officer Johnny Michael Spann was killed. He was the first US casualty of the war. Among the prisoners who survived was another American, John Walker Lindh. Later branded the "American Taliban," Lindh had been shot during the battle. As we were driving back to Rhino, Lindh was being flown down for medical treatment and interrogation.

Colonel Waldhauser had valid concerns for Lindh's safety. If it was discovered that he was in the camp and had been at least tangentially responsible for the death of a Marine, the likelihood of a "tragic accident" was high. So, Colonel Waldhauser turned to us. Not that we were less angry, but he knew we would carry out the mission. Captain Treglia met the aircraft on the runway under cover of darkness, took control of Lindh, and made sure that his wounds were treated, while the remainder of the platoon orchestrated the smoke and mirrors necessary to try to keep his presence a secret for as long as possible. Over the next several days, we kept guard over him during his detention and interrogation sessions, until he was transferred to the USS *Peleliu* on December 14. We wrapped up things at Rhino and were all back on ship shortly after the new year.

***

There are a million permutations of the statement, "There are two types of people, those who have _____ and those who haven't." With little fanfare, I had moved to the side of "those who have killed."

Sex is often used as an analogy for combat. A first firefight is called "popping one's cherry." It is an apt analogy. Both sex and killing are preceded by a buildup, worry, anticipation, and performance anxiety that (at least in my experience) far outweighs the reality. In both cases, it is over quickly, and you are left feeling different somehow, but not as you expected. It is as though a layer of skin had been shed or sloughed off, and the newly exposed skin is red and tender and each sensation that follows is felt as though it were the first time.

I was far more competent at killing for the first time than I had been at sex. I had practiced both alone with equal vigor, but with sex, I was left wondering if I had done everything right. With killing, there was little room for doubt.

With the killing, I was surprised because I felt, and still feel, nothing for those men. Sure, we were justified, seeking righteous retribution for the Towers, for New York, for America. That is a part of it. They were combatants, armed and able. We caught them off-guard. That was their fault. I'm sure they would admit to that. It was as fair as anything in war will ever be. But the truth I wasn't quite prepared for is that it is easy to kill. The seeming paradoxical truth was that while I felt absolute hatred for Lindh, I wouldn't have considered harming him.

I was brought up to believe in the sanctity of life, the divine spark that flickers and flares within each of us, and the horrible burden of shame that comes with extinguishing it. The grief Cain felt when he slew Able, the shame Moses experienced when he killed the Egyptian.

I felt relief that all my guys were safe. Pride that we had all performed well. But there was also an emptiness that comes when expectations are not met. I thought it would mean more or take some part of me. Maybe that was a part that was no longer there to take. An appendage that had been removed in the indoctrination of boot camp when we recited, "All I feel when I kill a gook is the recoil of my rifle, Sir!" Or sang a cadence while running, about luring a yellow bird to the windowsill to "smash its fucking head." Now I spend the better part of a small nation's GDP on bird seed and suet cakes and question the value of the song.

Or maybe it was an organ that atrophied and withered over years of training. I didn't spend a lot of mental energy on this at the time, but over the years I have returned to this question.

There was no elation at having killed, but there was a euphoria, the rush that comes with facing fight or flight and choosing fight. The chemical cocktail secreted that floods the body with cortisol, adrenaline, and dopamine, that makes you feel invincible and alters your perception of time and consciousness. When it is coursing through your veins, you *are* invincible, a god. If I am being honest, it's a good feeling. The kind that is easy to get addicted to.

CHAPTER 3

A BRIEF HISTORY OF MARINE SPECIAL OPERATIONS

*You cannot exaggerate about the Marines. They
are convinced to the point of arrogance that they
are the most ferocious fighters on earth. And
the amusing thing about it is that they are.*
—Navy Lieutenant Kevin Keaney, First Marine
Division chaplain during the Korean War

It is important to remember that the Marine Corps is a cult. The best kind of cult, I think, but a cult nevertheless. We have a saying, "Once a Marine, always a Marine." And those of us who have worn the Eagle, Globe, and Anchor see ourselves differently long after folding the uniform and relegating it to a footlocker stashed in the attic. This is true whether the Marine in question served one four-year enlistment, or thirty years.

We think of anyone who has not been a Marine as "not like us" and look upon anyone "not like us" with a mixture of mild scorn and pity. I still can't shake the feeling that for anyone who has not been a Marine there must be some twinge of sadness. Regret, deeply buried, seldom uncovered, but there even so, which emerges from time to time when a recruiting commercial plays on television, or when they spot a faded tattoo on an old man standing in the supermarket checkout line. While

I know plenty of people who have never been Marines and claim to be perfectly satisfied with their lives, I am unable to logically process how.

This indoctrination begins the moment a young man or woman is chased from a bus by the yells of a drill instructor. Everything that has transpired before that moment becomes irrelevant. B.C., Before the Corps.

In a lot of ways, my life began at seventeen with my first plane flight, then a bus ride through the tidal swamps along a winding causeway, to a set of yellow footprints painted on the sun-faded, cracked asphalt of Parris Island, South Carolina. We arrived at night, scrambling from the bus toward the spotlights and screams. The coastal humidity fell upon us like a heavy wet cloak, and the night smelled of salt air and fear as sand fleas in their legions descended, determined to suck every ounce of nasty civilian blood from us. We were stripped of everything that identified us—clothing, hair, even names. We each became "this recruit," while others became, "that recruit."

The early days. Sergeant Dailey on deployment in Korea as the Chief Scout Sniper with third battalion, seventh Marine Regiment. This is one of my few photos with the M-40A1 sniper rifle.

The ordinary world was left behind for the extraordinary world of Joseph Campbell's Monomyth. For thirteen weeks we endured trials and tribulations. Each of us, at some point, experienced an abyss of death and rebirth. Every future was possible, and the past, while ultimately irrelevant, became infinitely malleable because nobody knew you, knew who you were or what you had done before, and you could make it up as you went along.

The Marines have a thing called the buddy program, where you can join with a friend and go to boot camp together. But my platoon didn't have anyone that took advantage of it, so we were all free to invent whatever past we felt would serve us best. In recruit platoon 2076, of the sixty-three young men, nearly everyone claimed to be a state wrestling champ. And since we were all roughly the same age, and Parris Island only trains recruits from east of the Mississippi, the odds defied logic. The West Virginia contingent, of which I was a part, was large and apparently contained several state champs from the same year and weight class. But you didn't spend too much time trying to figure it out. There were so many other surreal realities to adjust to and plenty of other pressing matters to focus on.

I was too afraid of being caught in a lie, so I wouldn't claim a state wrestling title I hadn't earned, but will admit now to exaggerating my number of sexual conquests from zero to many.

I think it was less about lying than about rebecoming. Seizing the seldom-offered opportunity that complete anonymity offers to reinvent ourselves into the people we needed to be—to *become* the Marines we tried so hard to see ourselves as—and wanted so badly for everyone else to see us as.

And so, as Marines we view history differently. Our saga is a propaganda machine finely tuned to goad us forward when others retreat. An epic relayed with sound and fury by drill instructors well versed in the mantra, "Never let the truth get in the way of a good story."

I feel compelled to belabor this point, because for the remainder of this chapter, I will present a history of my Marine Corps and her involvement in Special Operations, as it was presented to me.

This account is more essential than history: it is legend, and as such, its absolute truth is far less important than its essence. This is what Tim O'Brien referred to in his seminal work, *The Things They Carried*, when he said that "story-truth is truer sometimes than happening-truth."

Boot Camp strips away allegiance and home, pimply faces and baby fat, and replaces them with loyalty to the Corps and Chesty Puller, smooth-shaved jaws and wiry muscles. It bends you like a sapling so far in one direction that although you may try to snap back when it is over, you will never quite return to center, and you will ever after lean distinctly toward the Southern Cross that our World War II Raider forefathers fought under. It is almost like a foreign country with a different clock and language, habits and hierarchy, customs and comrades, and new gods who demand nothing but total allegiance and offerings of blood.

When platoon 2076 marched across the graduation parade field on that bright, Indian-summer day in 1987, we were no longer in any part the boys that stepped off the bus three-plus months before. We had been replaced plank by plank, like Odysseus's ship, and were now and forever wholly Marine. Our ancestry now a direct lineage woven backwards to colonial barstools in Pennsylvania.

It is true that we were born in a bar, Tun Tavern in Philadelphia on November 10, 1775. By direction of the Continental Congress, two battalions of Marines were raised from among the clientele of Robert and Peggy Mullins's tavern and hot beefsteak house. These men were tasked with projecting the power of a fledgling nation across oceans. Marines, dependable and brave, served to protect the ship's captain— sometimes from his own sailors, who were occasionally less scrupulous. Marines climbed the rigging during ship-to-ship engagements, and with their superior marksmanship skills eliminated resistance as enemy vessels came alongside and clashed in naval battle. They led shore parties to raid fortifications and win glory.

In 1805 it was Lieutenant Presley O'Bannon and seven Marines who responded to the capture of the USS *Philadelphia* by Tripolean pirates under the orders of the pasha of Tripoli, Yusuf Karamanli. At the behest of President Thomas Jefferson, and working with the diplomat William Eaton, O'Bannon and his Marines debarked the USS *Argus* in Alexandria, Egypt to track down and enlist the support of the rightful but deposed ruler of Tripoli, Hamet Karamanli. Together with a force of five hundred men, including Arabs loyal to Hamet and paid mercenaries, the group began an arduous five-hundred-mile trek across the barren Libyan desert toward the port town of Derna. The eight Marines kept control, thwarting attempts at mutiny and desertion during the long march, arriving with the force on the night of April 25, 1805.

Following several days of intense fighting, O'Bannon led his men in a final charge to seize a strategic battery and turn its guns on the enemy. Here O'Bannon became the first to raise the American flag on foreign soil as he signaled to the United States ships *Nautilus*, *Argus*, and *Hornet* that the port was under American control. In gratitude, Hamet gifted O'Bannon a sword with a distinctive, jeweled Mameluke hilt. This blade was used as a model for the sword still carried by Marine officers today.

The courage of America's first special-operations mission is memorialized in the opening of "The Marines's Hymn": "*From the Halls of Montezuma to the shores of Tripoli.*" The lyrics are not chronological, as the "Halls of Montezuma" part happened forty-two years later, when Marines seized Chapultepec Castle during the Mexican-American War. And, strictly speaking, the castle was built 265 years after Montezuma was overthrown, but it makes for a rousing hymn. And I still can't hear it without straightening my back and lifting my chin a little bit.

Marines would continue to serve with distinction and win honors throughout the 1800s and in the Banana Wars of the early 1900s in Central America and the Caribbean. In China they put down the Boxer Rebellion; and on the fields of France during WWI, legend has it that they earned from the Germans the title *teufel hunden*, or "devil dogs," for their fighting tenacity.

But it wasn't until the bombing of Pearl Harbor in December 1941 that America began to recognize the requirement for dedicated special operations forces. President Roosevelt turned to the Marines and, predictably, the Marine Corps pushed back. The Marines have never liked to recognize an elite within the elite. In response to the proposal that the Marines develop a unit similar to the British Commandos, the Commandant of the Marine Corps, Major General Thomas Holcomb, retorted that "the term 'Marine' is sufficient to indicate a man ready for duty at any time, and the injection of a special name, such as 'Commando,' would be undesirable and superfluous."

But a believer in the commando concept, a young Marine captain named Jimmy Roosevelt, had the ear of his father, the president. Ultimately, the Marine Corps formed two battalions of Raiders (and later another two), tasked with small-unit operations behind enemy lines, wreaking havoc and destruction.

In one of the most daring raids of the war, on the night of August 17, 1942 the submarines USS *Argonaut* and *Nautilus* (the namesake of O'Bannon's ship) broke the surface a mile from the desolate Butaritari atoll, also known as Makin Island, part of the Gilbert Island chain. Led by their commander, Evans Carlson, the Raiders inflated rubber raiding boats and pushed off with small, unreliable, outboard engines puttering through the darkness. They made their way to shore and attacked the Japanese garrison. Due to the sheer audacity of the raid and the need to bolster American morale, a Hollywood production starring Randolph Scott and Robert Mitchum was soon filmed and given, as its title, the Raider motto: *Gung Ho!*

Over the next two years, Raiders would win battles and honors throughout the Pacific theatre, on the Solomon Island chain in places like Guadalcanal, Tulagi, New Georgia, and Bairoko Harbor earning valor awards that vastly outnumbered their size.

Second Platoon, First Force Recon Company with Brigadier General Mattis in early December 2001 at Camp Rhino.

In 1944, the Marine Corps disbanded her Raiders, relegating them to service in conventional infantry units where the veterans would continue to distinguish themselves for the remainder of the war in places like Guam and Okinawa. On Iwo Jima, two Raiders, Michael Strank and Harold Keller, were among the flag raisers memorialized in Joe Rosenthal's iconic photo.

It was also during the Pacific campaign that Marine amphibious reconnaissance was born. Recon Marines were trained to swim ashore at night, clad in swim trunks and carrying a fighting knife, to map beachheads and search for reefs and obstacles that could impede landing craft. They often operated in conjunction with Navy Underwater Demolition Team (UDT) frogmen who specialized in blowing up reefs to allow landing craft access. These Marines eventually would form the reconnaissance units I served with over forty years later, and the frogmen would evolve to be known by the acronym for their eventual operating environments: Sea, Air, and Land (SEAL).

While the Raiders were tearing up the Pacific theatre, another important unit was established. The Office of Strategic Services, or OSS, was founded at the direction of the president by William "Wild Bill" Donovan and was modeled after the newly formed British Special Operations Executive, or SOE. Though early discussions almost led to the appointment of Donovan as a Marine general tasked with developing a special operations force from within the Marines, Donovan's forces were the antithesis of the Raiders in many ways. While Raiders trained in the rugged coastal mountains and valleys of Southern California and the thick woods of Quantico, Virginia, OSS personnel often were selected from among blue bloods and frequently were housed in luxury. The OSS was tasked with covert operations: building networks of agents to get downed air crews safely out of enemy territory; supporting and building the resistance movements; conducting sabotage and subversion; and gathering and reporting information about enemy activities. Over seventy-five Marines served in the OSS, including actor Sterling Hayden. Captain Charlotte Gower, one of the first woman Marines to join the Corps in 1942, was the only female Marine to serve with the OSS and later the CIA, until her retirement in 1964.

The most famous OSS operative (at least to Marines) was Lieutenant Colonel Peter Ortiz. An adventurous blue blood, Ortiz spoke seven languages and had run away from his French boarding school to join the French Foreign Legion. He later returned to the United States to join the Marines as an enlisted man. When his capabilities and combat experience were discovered, he was posted to the OSS, promoted quickly to major, and sent to Africa to assist with planning for Operation Torch, the allied invasion of French North Africa.

He would later lead fellow Marines and others in the OSS team "Union II" in a night parachute jump into occupied France.

The tales of the OSS and Raider derring-do are bedtime stories Marines grow up with, but these tales seemed distant. A history to study and understand, but so far removed. Although I was too young to understand much of the Vietnam War while it was going on, I felt it was my war. As a teen, I was inundated with Vietnam movies starring Sylvester Stallone and Chuck Norris. I read memoirs and fiction of special operations teams on recon missions deep behind enemy lines and imagined myself among them. Even popular television shows like *Magnum P.I.* and *Simon and Simon* featured very special episodes where the cast was thrust into the jungles of Vietnam to rescue POWs. I salivated over the pages of *Soldier of Fortune* magazine and spent my free time in the woods trying to build skills that would serve me well. In high school I joined the cross-country, wrestling, and track teams to prepare myself.

Vietnam was also the next major inflection point for special operations. Marine reconnaissance teams evolved to conduct deep recon missions for battlespace-shaping, collecting and reporting information on enemy locations and troop movements, and executing surgical strikes deep in enemy territory.

Vietnam produced recon legends like Don Hamblen, who despite losing his leg below the knee in a parachute accident, completed two combat tours. James Capers, leader of Team Broadminded, who led sixty-four long-range reconnaissance patrols. Capers was promoted from the ranks and was the first African American to receive a battlefield commission, and the first to command a recon company. John Ripley, who almost singlehandedly held off an NVA tank battalion by swinging hand over hand along the length of the bridge at Dong Ha to place explosives while under fire, destroying the bridge. And Jimmie Howard, whose eighteen-man recon team held off a three-hundred-man NVA battalion through a hellish night assault. With grenades spent and ammo running low, the survivors took to throwing rocks at the human waves that repeatedly broke against the Marines' tight defensive perimeter. When the sun rose over Hill 488 the next morning, six of Howard's men were dead, all were wounded, but the attack had been repulsed. The recovery force which arrived later in the day to extract the team counted two hundred NVA dead. Howard received the Medal of Honor and his third Purple Heart. His team earned four Navy Crosses and thirteen Silver Stars (the second- and third-highest valor awards, respectively).

While Recon Marines were making names for themselves, Navy SEALs were striking targets in and around the coastline and waterways, and Army Special Forces (Green Berets) were building and training partisan forces among the Montagnards of the central highlands, the Nungs of Northern Vietnam, and South Vietnamese forces.

Select members from all these special operations units were hand-picked to work together under the Military Assistance Command, Vietnam–Studies and Observations Group (MACV-SOG). Often working at the behest of the CIA, these teams operated covertly across Vietnam and into Laos and Cambodia. I have the great honor of calling one of these men, John Stryker "Tilt" Meyer, a friend. Tilt, an Army Special Forces soldier, spent two tours of duty with SOG in Vietnam. Listening to his stories reminds me that while the methods for waging warfare have changed greatly over the years, strong backs, hard feet, and a dedication to one's comrades has always been and will always be a prerequisite.

But despite the successes and stellar reputation of her Recon Marines, following Vietnam the Marine Corps deactivated First Force Reconnaissance Company, only reactivating it 1987.

Shipboard training with First Force Reconnaissance Company. We were required to shoot every few days to retain our hostage rescue qualification.

There has always been a distinct interservice rivalry among the branches, and nowhere is this more prevalent than among SOF (even though Recon Marines are clearly superior). But institutional jealousy aside, until this time, all special operations units were on relatively similar footing. The events that would eventually change this began on the morning of April 4, 1979, when a group of militant college students assaulted the US Embassy in Teheran, Iran and seized fifty-two American hostages.

My memories of the hostage crisis are hazy—I was ten. I have vague recollections of Ed Bradley and Dan Rather discussing the hostages' plight as I switched between the four available TV channels. But I do remember sitting with my cousin Butch, fishing from a stone bridge near my home, our Zebco 77s baited with night crawlers, bottles of grape Nehi sweating in the shade, and my blue, nine-volt-powered transistor radio with its silver antenna extended and canted to catch a signal—when I heard what I thought were the opening lyrics to the Beach Boys' *Barbara Ann*. It took a few moments to realize that we were hearing a parody by Vince Vance & the Valiants: *Bomb Iran*.

While my understanding of the political situation remained limited, I have never been able to listen to the Beach Boys the same way again.

Negotiations for the hostages' release were at a stalemate, so a risky joint special operations mission was conceived to free them. On April 24, 1980, men from a unit led by Colonel Charlie Beckwith rendezvoused prior to the planned assault with navy helicopters piloted by Marines at a small desert airstrip dubbed "Desert One." When a helicopter collided with a transport aircraft carrying men and fuel, eight service members were killed and the rescue mission was aborted.

In response to the mission's failure, the Joint Chiefs of Staff launched an investigation led by retired Admiral James Holloway. The Holloway report pointed to deficiencies in mission planning, command and control, and issues with interservice operability.

In 1986, the Goldwater-Nichols Act led to the creation of unified combatant commands to streamline chains of command along geographic regions. Goldwater-Nichols also suggested the creation of a service-like special operations command. This suggestion was ignored until 1988 when Senators Sam Nunn and William Cohen introduced the Nunn-Cohen Amendment which, when ratified, directed the formation of the United States Special Operations Command (USSOCOM).

On April 16, 1987, USSOCOM was established at MacDill Air Force Base in Florida. Units from the army, Special Forces, Rangers, and a special ops helicopter squadron were placed under the new organization. The air force contributed special operations aircraft, para-rescue, and combat-controller units, and the navy provided its SEALs under the newly formed Naval Special Warfare Command.

In a predictable move, the Marine Corps opted out of providing forces. The Marine Corps commandant, General Paul X. Kelly, instead refocused the entire Marine Corps toward its expeditionary roots. The former Marine Amphibious Unit was redesignated as the Marine Expeditionary Unit (Special Operations Capable), or MEU SOC. The MEU SOC, supported by naval shipping, was a purpose-built Marine Air-Ground Taskforce, or MAGTF.

Two MEU SOCs originating from each of the East and West Coast Marine Expeditionary Forces conducted overlapping six-month deployments, designed to provide a persistent presence around the globe and serve as a rapid-response force. They were tasked with executing thirteen special operations, including in-extremis hostage rescue, gas-and-oil platform seizure, maritime interdiction operations, and deep reconnaissance. The responsibility for the bulk of these operations fell to the ad hoc organization dubbed the Maritime Special Purpose Force (MSPF), with the Force Recon platoon at its core.

While all of this was taking place, I was graduating from high school and, in July of 1987, shipping off to boot camp. Following boot camp, while attending infantry training, I was given my first opportunity to try out for recon. Unfortunately, while I was in great shape overall, my swimming skills were nowhere close to where they needed to be. I had grown up jumping into creeks and ponds and was confident in my ability to stay afloat, but when challenged to demonstrate actual swimming strokes, or to rescue a drowning victim, I failed to meet the required standard. And so, I was assigned to the Third Battalion, Seventh Marine Regiment in Camp Pendleton, California.

In the Marine Corps, your job is referred to by a four-number code that indicates your Military Occupational Specialty, or MOS. If you are in the infantry, that MOS begins with 03. This is followed by two numbers designating your specialty. For example, I was an 0311 Infantryman. An 0331 is a machine gunner, an 0341 is a mortar man, etc. While checking in, a clerical error changed the course of my life.

I reported to the clerk at the desk, handed him my orders, and he directed me to report to Weapons Company. He made this announcement as his heavy stamp thudded, leaving an indelible punctuation to his proclamation. I joined the procession of sea-bag-dragging Marines making their way across the parade ground to the company offices, and I found the door marked "Weapons." As we had been taught, I pounded my open palm three times on the door and waited for the command to enter. At a desk sat a giant of a man wearing the rank that I had never seen, only heard about: first sergeant. Now the thing about first sergeants is that they only do three things, but they do them all very well. They smoke, drink coffee, and yell at people—especially PFCs like me, and especially when said PFC was apparently interrupting something of the utmost importance, which I could only presume was either smoking or drinking coffee. As he looked at my orders he remarked, "There must be some mistake. This says you are an 0311. We don't have 0311s in Weapons Company. You must be an 0331. Report to Heavy Machine Guns Platoon."

"But First Sergeant, I am an 0311."

"You can't be an 0311, we don't have 0311s in Weapons Company, I told you. What company are you in?"

"Weapons Company?"

"God damn right, and are there 0311s in Weapons Company?"

"No, First Sergeant."

"Then how in the hell could you be an 0311?"

I found myself beginning to follow his logic and started to move toward the door when I remembered a crucial bit of information. I knew nothing about machine guns. So, I finally withdrew the graduation certificate from among my records and presented it to the now smoking and coffee-drinking first sergeant. After a five-minute torrent of obscenities directed at me, he arrived at a Solomon-like decision. It would be a pain in the ass to get the error corrected; therefore, it was easier to assign me to the only place in Weapons Company that they could possibly assign an 0311: the Surveillance and Target Acquisition (STA) Platoon. I didn't know what a STA platoon was, but imagined it must be vastly preferable to the first sergeant's office, and readily agreed. Another clerk was tasked to escort me to meet the STA platoon sergeant. Upon arriving at the platoon office, I was greeted...greeted is probably not the right word. "Screamed at for no good reason" is probably a bit more accurate.

STA Platoon was where the snipers were. In the Marine Corps, snipers hold an almost mythological status. All Marines revere marksmanship and place incredible value on those who excel at it, but to be a sniper much more is required. It is not enough to be able to shoot well. You also must be able to live off of the land, operating far in advance of friendly forces and usually in a two-man team. In this case, invisibility is your best defense. This is why only the best, most experienced Marines from the battalion were allowed even to try out for the sniper platoon. The tryout took place once a year and could last for up to thirty days. There were limited openings, and these were hotly contested within each unit. Most applicants would quit or be cut before the course completion, but even those who survived were not guaranteed a slot in the platoon.

Guess who jumped the line? You can imagine the warm reception that I received. And why the platoon sergeant was so happy to see me.

Fortunately, I was eventually able to win the platoon over and complete sniper school. A few years later, I volunteered for assignment abroad and worked at the embassies in Budapest, Hungary and Buenos Aires, Argentina before returning to the States and getting another opportunity to try out for Force Recon in 1994.

CHAPTER 4
PLANK OWNERS

*Realizing it is my choice and my choice alone
to be a Reconnaissance Marine, I accept all
challenges involved with this profession. Forever
shall I strive to maintain the tremendous
reputation of those who went before me.*
—First stanza of "The Recon Creed"

I t was the end of March 2002 when the ships brought us home from Afghanistan. The evening before we arrived, they anchored a mile off the coast. The smell of Camp Pendleton's wild fennel was like black licorice in our noses, and that smell brought with it memories of home that made the final night almost unbearable. I lived in a house on base, and from the flight deck of the USS *Peleliu* I could see the tan walls and terra cotta tiles of the Stuart Mesa housing area even if I could not identify my house.

GySgt. J.A DAILEY
HILLSBOROUGH, VA.
1ST FORCE RECON 2ND PLT
15TH MEU

SSGT. M.D. FAY USMCR

**This sketch was made by combat artist Michael Fay during a
debrief aboard the USS *Peleliu* shortly after leaving Afghanistan.
He captured the weariness that comes with combat.**

I could picture Tracy cooking dinner, Garrett and Kallie playing with friends in the quiet streets and interconnected backyards until it was time to eat. This was the way it was.

The starboard side rail was jammed with Marines and sailors bitching about being so close yet having to wait until tomorrow to begin the offload. Some contemplated jumping over the rail. Could they make the swim? How much trouble would they get into? Would it be worth it?

My platoon was fortunate to be on an early helicopter flight, while some would wait all day for landing craft sorties that wouldn't arrive until evening. Still others, those without spouses or children or significant others, would ride the boats back to port in San Diego to keep an eye on equipment that wouldn't be retrieved until later in the week.

On military bases someone is always going or coming. Families dress up and show up to hug and kiss and cry tears of sadness or joy. This return was different, though. We were returning from a war that didn't exist when we left, and so we came home to greater fanfare. Signs crafted from posterboard or bedsheets adorned garage doors and fences, welcoming units or individual Marines. Red solo cups crammed into chain-link fences spelled out well-wishes in block letters.

Each departure following our return would have a different meaning. As the buses pulled away, it would be with the knowledge that loved ones were going to war. And for far too many, it would end early, with a government car slowly pulling up to a house, and a uniformed officer and chaplain making the slow and somber trudge to a doorway. Children quickly learned to race home to notify their parents at the sight of a white sedan with government plates. The street would hold its collective breath, willing the vehicle to continue to another block. Each return from deployment would be sweeter for those who made it, but it is easy to feel that each return loads another round in another cylinder of the roulette revolver.

Returning from deployment is always a shock to the system. To several systems, really. First, there is just being back in the States, the land of the big PX. You can largely get what you want when you want, but in exchange you return to polite company. Jokes and comments that were funny while cooped up on ship aren't always funny now. The second shock is to reintroduce yourself into a family that has been functioning without you for six or seven months. Sure, they missed you and you them, but they have lives to live, schedules have been established, and rules adhered to.

Tracy is a master of schedules, while despite my years of military training I remain a fly-by-the-seat-of-my-pants guy. But I had learned that returning, while joyous, causes upheaval, and sticking to schedules helps to dampen the changes.

Children grow so much in seven months. The time, which for me was fleeting, barely a half-trip around the sun, makes up a greater percentage of their short lives. So much changes for them and with them in that span of time. Garrett was nearly eight and Kallie almost five. Her kindergarten class, which hadn't begun when I left, was now nearly over.

Tracy and I attending a USMC birthday celebration in 1996.

Before going on deployment in 2001, Tracy and I discussed requesting assignment to embassy duty upon return. This would mean three years overseas with my family without worrying about separation. I met Tracy when I worked as an embassy guard in Budapest in 1989. She had travelled there after college with an aunt and uncle who worked at the embassy, and she found work as a schoolteacher. Now, she looked forward again to the experience abroad, for our children as well as the steady schedule for me. If I returned, I would be the detachment commander, responsible for the embassy's Marine contingent. It would be a great job offering autonomy and normal office hours.

We sat down and discussed it now. I steered the conversation to the unknown, to the dangers of living abroad, especially with kids. To the unpredictability of a post-9/11 world. This was all true, but I also couldn't take an assignment that would remove my opportunity to return to war. And, while I had enjoyed the time I spent on embassy duty, I had found a brotherhood amongst Recon Marines I couldn't imagine leaving.

At this same time, my commander at First Force Recon, Colonel Robert Coates, was reassigned as the commander of the First Special Operations Training Group (SOTG). He asked if I would be interested in taking over the Reconnaissance and Surveillance (R&S) section, where I would be responsible for running the urban sniper and reconnaissance courses.

It seemed like the perfect compromise. I would be able to help train Marines for combat and pass on what I knew, while I worked on building my own skills and preparing for an opportunity to return to war.

The Marine Corps is an incubator for rumors. There are always several floating around, said to originate from "the third shitter to the left," which if brought to fruition would change the course of life as we knew it. It was about this time that a rumor started circulating that the Marine Corps was going to develop a unit to be assigned to SOCOM. Because it was rumor, it was largely ignored but not squashed.

I threw myself into the job at SOTG. I was able to bring Glen and T.C. with me from my platoon. Along with a few other First Force alum, we made up an almost-new cadre. I like to start from scratch without being bogged down in the way things used to be, especially if we were to prepare Marines for the war to come.

SOTG conducted training courses and evaluated training exercises to prepare the members of a Marine Expeditionary Unit for deployment and to qualify them as Special Operations Capable (MEU SOC). The urban sniper course focused on precision shooting at night in challenging urban environments. It required extreme accuracy and the ability to calculate bullet drop over the trajectory of the round's flight. This enabled shooters to ensure that their shots would not be thrown off by powerlines or bridges along the bullets' paths.

The Urban R&S course trained the Marines from the Reconnaissance Battalion and a radio recon detachment that provided signals intelligence support, to conduct reconnaissance and surveillance operations in urban areas in support of the Force platoon's direct-action missions.

For the uninitiated, the distinction between Recon Battalion and Force Recon may require a word of explanation. While sharing the same baseline capabilities, Recon Battalion provides support at the Marine division level, conducting reconnaissance and collecting information for the assigned unit commander. Force Reconnaissance works for the Marine Air-Ground Task Force commander, and frequently operates deeper behind enemy lines. Force Recon teams also have the mission of serving as the direct-action capability for the MEU and are largely responsible for the associated missions of In-extremis Hostage Rescue (IHR), Gas and Oil Platform (GOPLAT) Seizure, and underway ship Visit, Board, Search, and Seizure (VBSS). Often Marines will start their career in Recon Battalion, then progress to Force Recon, bouncing back and forth to fill positions of increased leadership responsibility throughout a career.

We taught them photography; techniques for establishing communication from within buildings; methods of transmitting detailed data on the makeup of the building, entries, and vulnerabilities; reporting on enemy pattern of life and habits; and establishing observation posts in urban areas. During training, the teams would spend weeks living in crappy L.A. hotel rooms, observing and reporting on abandoned buildings manned by our role players.

To the curriculum I added pistol marksmanship from concealed carry, hand-to-hand combat training, lock-picking, and urban evasion. It was obvious that we had for so long trained for deployments consisting only of more training, that we had let the lessons of combat slip. Recon teams of four to six men, or sniper teams of two, are incredibly vulnerable. While in a perfect world they will slip in, accomplish the mission, and slip out unseen—and that is what we train for—we need to prepare them for the worst.

I loved it. I still worked long hours and traveled frequently, but I was home most evenings and weekends. I was able to attend school events and take Garrett and Kallie to activities on the weekends. It was around this time, while attending the debriefing for one of our pre-deployment exercises, that Colonel Coates approached me.

"Ranger, you've heard the rumors about the SOCOM unit?"

"Yes, Sir. Any truth to them?"

He nodded. "They've asked me to lead it. You want in?"

I have no idea how I even replied. It was in the affirmative, but I can't recall if I just nodded, or squealed like a little girl. It was the equivalent of a guitarist being asked, "Hey, do you want to join the Foo Fighters?" Or a farm-club player being asked, "Do you feel like pitching a World Series game?"

Coates slapped me on the back and said, "Keep it under your hat for now. I'll let you know more."

***

I had received the nickname "Ranger" shortly after arriving at First Force Recon in 1994. In the two years between embassy duty and getting to Force Recon, I had been re-assigned to the Third Battalion, Seventh Marine Regiment. This was where I had started my military career, but in the years since I left, they had moved from Camp Pendleton on the beautiful California coast to Twenty-Nine Palms, California, a backwater desert town in the Mojave Desert. At that time, Tracy and I were in a long-distance relationship, with her in Pittsburgh,

Pennsylvania. I was assigned as the chief sniper for the 3/7 Surveillance and Target Acquisition platoon.

Shortly after arriving in Twenty-Nine Palms, we were notified that a small number of quotas were available to attend the US Army Ranger school. I didn't know much about it, other than it was hard, and I have generally operated under the assumption that if it is hard, it must be good.

So, I tried out and was eventually able to attend the course. Ranger school largely consists of starving and being sleep-deprived while patrolling around in environments ranging from swamps to mountains to deserts. Along the way, you are occasionally thrust into leadership positions and expected to cajole, motivate, or threaten your teammates, who are also starving and sleep-deprived, into doing what you need them to do. I was successful enough to graduate, and for my sins was sent to Army Airborne School.

With me being back east for the school, Tracy and I used the opportunity to get a quick justice-of-the-peace wedding, although we would continue to live separately for nearly a year as I trained and prepared for a deployment that took me to Okinawa, Japan.

Following that deployment, and the church wedding we had promised our parents, I brought Tracy out to Twenty-Nine Palms, where she was introduced to the real Marine Corps. Her knowledge of what I did had been limited to seeing me in uniform or in a suit around the embassy, or attending cocktail parties and elaborate Marine Corps Birthday Balls. The reality of living far from civilization, in a tiny house in the desert with coyotes wandering through the front yard, came as a shock; but she took it in stride and began working at a preschool in town.

But blessedly, our stay together in Twenty-Nine Palms was short, as the desert was mercilessly hot and now Tracy was sweating for two. I had spent as much of the deployment as possible preparing for the First Force Recon Indoctrination, or "Indoc," and so as soon as I could, I made the move and tried out.

The Force Indoc was a single-day event and was mostly physical. I arrived long before sunup and joined a group of fellow Marines in an open parking lot dressed in green running shorts and T-shirts. Eventually, a sergeant came around to take down our names and collect the paperwork we each clutched in sweaty palms. Few of the men knew each other. Some congregated in small groups; others, like myself, stood alone. We all eyed each other, trying to size up the competition.

Just as the sun was rising, the cadre emerged from the building. The senior man gave a brief of the first event, the Marine Corps physical fitness test (PFT), which consisted of pull-ups, sit-ups, and a three-mile run. A perfect score was expected.

After the PFT, we were led on a long run that eventually ended at the swimming pool, and we changed into full camouflage uniforms. For the next several hours, cadre members with stopwatches called out strokes and recorded times: five-hundred-meter sidestroke, underwater crossovers, water-tread while passing bricks back and forth, jumping from the thirty-foot tower to retrieve a rifle from the bottom of the pool.

From the pool we ran again, miles, still soaking wet. We reached an obstacle course, which was completed many times. Then another run back to the parking lot, where our fifty-pound rucks were waiting. By now we were nearly dry. We rucked up and took off, following the signs that pointed into the hills. There was no talking, no encouragement, no idea of how long the route was or how much time we had to complete it. We went for hours through the hills of coastal California, then down to the soft sand before they told us to stop. Then into the ocean, choking down salt water and doing exercises in the surf zone. That's when people started to quit. Once one quits, it becomes contagious, the Black Death. Finally, soaked and with sand in all the places you don't want sand, we rucked back up and headed back into the hills.

By now there were only a few still going. A truck followed along behind. No one tried to stop those who got in. We had started with twenty-some. Five of us finished the physical part.

Then the testing started: psychological, intelligence, temperament. Finally, the interview. "Why do you want to do this?" "What are some of your favorite books?" "What's your opinion on the political situation in the Philippines?" Then the scenario:

"You are leading a team conducting a desert observation post overlooking a village, and a shepherd discovers your location. You can let him go and abort the mission, or kill him. What do you do, Dailey?"

"I don't know what I'd do," I said. "I'd have to understand the situation, the criticality of the mission. I don't think those are the only two options."

Only two of us were selected.

When I checked in, I was put to work in the Operations section while I waited for a coveted spot in a platoon. While I was there, a staff sergeant who would grow to become my mentor and trusted friend, nicknamed Willy-T, asked about my background. I told him about my time as a sniper. He seemed impressed that I had been to Ranger school. After our conversation, he began to advocate for me to join his platoon, but couldn't remember my name, so he just called me "the Ranger." The name stuck. I still turn my head if I hear it today.

CHAPTER 5

STRONG BACKS AND HARD FEET

All it takes is all you've got.
—Gunnery Sergeant Christopher Antonik,
First Marine Raider Battalion KIA 7/11/2010

Finally, on a Monday, Colonel Coates notified me that the unit was forming. We would be called Marine Corps Special Operations Command Detachment One. Abbreviated to MCSOCOM Det-One. But quickly we just went by Det-One, or just "the Det."

Our beginnings were inauspicious. Those of us that worked for SOTG simply began working two jobs. Initially we had few people, no buildings or equipment, and little to do. So we spent a lot of time in the gym, and began working on developing standard operating procedures, or SOPs.

We were to be eighty-six men strong in a small headquarters organized around the war-fighting functions of Command, Operations, Administration, Logistics, Communications, and Maintenance; a robust recon/assault platoon; a similarly robust intelligence platoon; and a small fires cell.

In the beginning, the recon/assault platoon was organized into four teams composed of six Marines and one Navy Special Amphibious Reconnaissance Corpsman. Coates pulled me and Joe from SOTG to lead teams. Terry came from First Force and Chunks from the Mountain Warfare Training Center. Coates called each of us into his office separately and presented his expectations.

Once again, celebrating a Marine Corps birthday with Detachment One. From left to right: Captain Eric Thompson, Me, Terry, Chunks, Joe, (the original four team leaders) and Keith. (Several faces have been obscured for security.)

Even though I had known Coates for years and truly respected and admired him, I was always nervous loitering around in the hall in front of his office. When the door opened, he just barked, "Ranger."

I walked in. "Good morning, Sir."

"Shut the door, sit down."

The floor of Coates's office was dominated by a Soviet-era Afghan rug that I had admired for years—called a "War rug," and made by the Afghan people. Woven into the fabric were images of Russian tanks, AK-47s, and Hind helicopters. When I was in Afghanistan in 2001, I had the chance to acquire a similar rug and didn't hesitate. It now covers the floor in my office. Several framed pictures of Coates, then a captain, hung on the walls. In one he sat in the open door of a Huey helicopter—not the barrel-chested man I knew, but long-haired and rail-thin from patrolling the jungles of El Salvador, where he had spent the late '80s working as an advisor, participating in operations against the Farabundo Martí National Liberation Front (FMLN).

"OK, Ranger, I'm giving you a team. You know what I expect—excellence."

"Yes, Sir."

"You pick your guys, and we'll try to get 'em. I want tough, rugged bastards with strong backs and hard feet."

"I've got a couple of guys in mind, Sir."

"I'm thinking of bringing back Mike and Eric," two Marines who had left the Marine Corps from First Force Recon. "What do you think?"

"I'd take either or both. I'd like to get Sid as my ATL" [Assistant Team Leader]."

"You're not the only one that wants him, but you two have known each other for years, haven't you?"

"Yes, Sir, we were in 3/7 together years ago."

"Alright, you've got him."

"How about Bo and Ben?"

"They're still deployed, but we can grab them when they get back. Have you worked with Doc Arnold?"

"I haven't, but his reputation's good. If he's onboard, I'll take him."

"Good. I'm going to want you to take the lead on sniping and work on building the equipment issue. Jon Laplume at Natick is going to be helping with gear; you two know each other."

"Yes, Sir, be good to see him again."

"Alright. Get to work."

I stood. "Roger that. Good morning, Sir." I turned and walked back out.

One of the countless leadership lessons that I learned from Colonel Coates was to give guidance that is as specific as necessary but as broad as possible. This invites creativity, builds problem-solving, and engenders a sense of ownership of the mission or task. All of this, combined, fueled a drive to complete each task to the highest standard possible, which is what he demanded.

The Det officially activated in a small ceremony on June 20, 2003, but in the months before that, beginning in February, we did what we could. Temporary buildings were constructed on a small, open piece of land beside the boat basin on Camp Del Mar, the southernmost corner of Camp Pendleton: three sprung structures, little more than rubber-coated nylon pulled tight over a framework of metal ribs.

Sid, my ATL, had been working in the CQB (close-quarters battle) section at SOTG after a long stay at First Force. While we were in 3/7 on our last Okinawa deployment, we worked out together to get ready for the Force Indoc. I was lucky to get him. Coates worked some magic to get Mike and Eric back in the Marine Corps. Both had gotten out. Mike moved his family home to Pittsburgh and Eric bummed around California racing motorcycles. Neither were terribly impressed with civilian life.

As Marines began trickling in, we worked out. There wasn't much else to do at first. We went on long runs down the beach or out through the streets of Oceanside, and loaded packs and hiked through the soft sand, strengthening our backs and hardening our feet.

I took several trips to Natick Labs just outside of Boston. Natick is the army research facility where everything from boots to body armor to field rations are invented and tested. Jon Laplume was a former Army Ranger who had jumped into Panama in 1989. He was now working in the special operations equipment section at Natick. Jon had helped us develop a new equipment suite following a terrible helicopter accident in December 1999.

On that grim day, Fifth Platoon from First Force was conducting a rehearsal for a maritime vessel takedown called a VBSS, or Visit, Board, Search, and Seizure. This was a mission undertaken to take control of a ship at sea. It involved rapidly getting forces onto the ship in two ways: from surface-up, by approaching in small boats and using grappling hooks to hook and climb, and/or from top-down, by fast-roping down onto the deck from helicopters. Teams would then maneuver to seize control of the key spaces necessary to control the ship: the bridge, aft steering, and the captain's cabin. Once the bridge and aft steering are controlled, you control the maneuvering of the vessel, and once you control the captain, you can usually control the crew.

In this exercise, the SEALs were assaulting from surface-up, by approaching the vessel in small, rigid-hull inflatable boats (RHIBs). They were responsible for hooking metal caving ladders at points on the ship's railing and climbing aboard, while our guys came in from top-down. The pilot for the lead helicopter came in low from the rear of the ship to hide his approach, but he misjudged his height. The helicopter skid snagged the safety net running along the side of the ship. When he attempted to correct, the helo rolled into the ocean, with Recon men and aircrew scrambling to fight their way out of the rapidly sinking aircraft as it filled with cold, black water. The helo eventually came to rest at a depth of over 3,600 feet of seawater, taking with it Recon men Staff Sergeant Vince Sabasteanski, Staff Sergeant David Galloway, Staff Sergeant Jeffrey Starling, Corporal Mark Baca, Recon Corpsman HM1 Jay Asis, and the helicopter crew chief, Gunnery Sergeant James Paige.

The crash was caused by pilot error, but factors contributing to the deaths were the weight of equipment, inadequacy of the flotation devices, and lack of supplemental oxygen. In the aftermath of the crash, the Marine Corps convened a small working group to address the issue. I represented First Force Recon. I was honored to be able to do something that I hoped would prevent a similar tragedy in the future. For several weeks we pieced together an integrated equipment set that included lighter-weight, more-robust ballistic protection, with equipment pouches that provided greater modularity, a flotation device that would do a better job of pulling Marines to the surface, and a spare air bottle that provided enough oxygen to help a struggling Marine get to an aircraft exit and make it to the surface with a smaller, communication-integrated helmet. The suite of equipment came to be known as Full Spectrum Battle Equipment, or FSBE for short.

Now I was back at Natick labs redesigning the Det-One equipment suite with Laplume. There had been advances in ballistic plate technology, making them lighter, thinner. We changed the color from woodland camouflage to a coyote tan, added newer night-vision mounts for the helmets, and increased the modularity and quantity of pouches to match anticipated mission requirements.

While I focused on personal protective equipment, other Marines were visiting manufacturers building weapons to specifications. We purchased commercial off-the-shelf Kimber .45 caliber pistols modified to meet our needs. An after-market Dawson Precision rail was added to attach a pistol light. We purchased accessories and scope mounts from Mark LaRue in Texas; glasses, goggles, and boots from Oakley; and rifle suppressors and weapons' lights from Sure Fire. Much of our tactical nylon gear was made for us by Eagle Industries, a brand with a stellar reputation for excellence. Local knife-maker Strider Knives created a custom folding knife.

The temporary structures were finally completed, and the unit was filling up with boxes and office furniture. But while we waited for enough personnel and equipment to really begin training, the one thing we could do was ruck.

Rucking under load for long distances over rugged terrain is, in my opinion, the best way to develop both overall conditioning and mental toughness. Every muscle works to progress forward and stabilize the load, while the ups and downs and flats challenge the system differently. To continue when you don't feel you can, pushes you past the boundaries of comfort and makes pain an ally. This is what Coates meant by strong backs and hard feet. Being comfortable in discomfort. Psychologists call it stress inoculation.

I've often wondered what all of us had in common, what brought us all from disparate backgrounds and made us successful in Recon. At the heart of it, we simply refused to quit, for long enough to allow us to build a reservoir of inner strength. Strong backs and hard feet don't guarantee success; but the willingness to build them, and the resignation to a fate of being tired, wet, cold, and hungry certainly does.

We were trained to maintain equanimity, to get through situations using our head when it was possible, or unrelenting violence when it was not. The ability to remain calm was instilled through stress inoculation, built into all our training. In our combatant dive school, it began with an event called sharking.

**My only photo of dive school. My dive buddy and I in the early
stages of getting "sharked." (I'm the one on the left.)**

We swam as two-man teams in circles along the bottom of a twen-
ty-foot-deep saltwater pool, waiting.

Rule number one is: *never leave your buddy*. It comes without warning: two instructors attack, rip your mouthpieces out, turn off the air,
pull your masks away and toss them. Saltwater burns your eyes and
forces its way up your noses. They take your weight belts and fins and
scatter them across the bottom of the pool. Then they tie your air hoses
into elaborate knots and turn the air back on, which pressurizes the
hose. It stiffens the hose, tightening the knots.

Rule number two is: *never lose your air tanks*. They pull at the straps,
try to tear them away as you tumble across the bottom. You're screwed
if you lose them, so you grip the nylon straps with all your might, curl
up in a ball and take your beating, holding your breath and waiting for
it to stop.

Finally, it does—and this is the crucial time. You choke back
panic. White sparkles appear at the corners of your eyes. You know
these come first: soon your vision will begin to tunnel, the blackness

collapsing from the periphery inward until you black out, but you resist the urge to bolt for the surface. You can see it, the light above, but that would be failure. You focus on the problem and do the counterintuitive: feel for the knob at the top of the air tank and turn it off, follow the tangled, knotted hose with your hand until you reach the regulator, put the snarled mouthpiece in your mouth and expel the little air remaining in your burning lungs to clear it. You suck in water and get a half-breath from the knotted hose, and that releases the pressure. Now you can work to untie the knots. Your chest is heaving; carbon dioxide sits like a burning black weight in your lungs. You fumble with tingling fingers to get purchase on the slick rubber of the hose until the knots are cleared. Now you can turn the air back on; now you can breathe.

With the first deep breath, the encroaching blackness vanishes. The breathing steadies and slows. Now you can figure out what you need to do next: find your mask, put it on, and tilt your head back and press the top of the mask tight against your forehead, exhale through your nose to clear the water out, find your fins, put them on, then your weight belt, then get your tank straps back around your shoulders, then see if you can help your buddy. It sucks bad, but each time you're more confident in your ability to save yourself. The message is clear: take one problem at a time, solve it, then move to the next.

I kept the poem *If* by Rudyard Kipling taped to my mirror during Combatant Dive School:

> *If you can keep your head when all about you*
> *Are losing theirs and blaming it on you;*
> *If you can trust yourself when all men doubt you,*
> *But make allowance for their doubting too...*

You need to keep your head to keep control of your breathing. When the fight-or-flight response kicks in, if you can control your breathing, you can control your heart rate, and then you can control your thinking when things suddenly go to shit. The amygdala and the hypothalamus sit in the middle of the brain. When the amygdala is alerted to a potentially dangerous situation, it calls on the hypothalamus to produce a chemical cocktail that stimulates the adrenal glands into releasing cortisol and adrenaline into the bloodstream. Cortisol increases the glucose in the blood, hyper-fueling muscle and feeding the brain. Adrenaline spikes the heart rate, increasing respiration to attempt to take in more oxygen. Blood shunts away from the extremities and gets stored in large muscles, preparing the body to either fight or flee. Pupils dilate to take in more light, also making it difficult to focus. Fine motor skills deteriorate, impacting hand-eye coordination. For the uninitiated, this series of survival mechanisms can seem catastrophic, which can allow fear to spawn panic.

When this happens, the three things we needed to do most precisely—think, see, and shoot—become nearly impossible. So, we prepared relentlessly, religiously. Our training was designed to put us under as much stress as possible and force us to make decisions. During our Survival Evasion Resistance and Escape (SERE) course: can you keep calm while being waterboarded? (Not for very long.) What do you do after a five-day desert patrol when you're out of food and water, and the helicopter that's supposed to pick you up drops a note with a new extract point on the other side of a mountain? Can you deal with a parachute malfunction at thirty thousand feet in the pitch black? You have the rest of your life to figure it out.

At the time, I didn't recognize how much of our training was designed to develop and strengthen mental toughness and resilience because the mechanism used was always physical. We valued the ability to make good decisions under pressure, but we strove for and admired hardness.

The greatest compliment that one Recon Marine could pay another was to describe him as "hard."

"Do you know Sid?"

"Yeah, he's a good guy, fucking hard."

That would be followed by a head nod. We knew what that meant, there was no need to elaborate or clarify. Hardness was the Recon Good Housekeeping Seal of Approval. It was an amalgamation of the physical and mental qualities that personified the ideal teammate. But hardness came at the expense of chipping away all unnecessary material through repeated forging. Time between hammer and anvil.

However, when you chip away everything that is not Recon Marine, essential parts of humanity can be left on the floor: compassion, empathy, emotion. They can be easier to divest than to hide.

A portion of "The Recon Creed" says it like this: "Conquering all obstacles, both large and small, I shall never quit. To quit, to surrender, to give up is to fail. To be a Recon Marine is to surpass failure; to overcome, to adapt and to do whatever it takes to complete the mission…"

And so, early each Thursday morning we were driven to a dirt lot near the First Force compound and dropped off. Before our equipment came in, we hiked in whatever rucks we owned, loaded with fifty pounds of dry weight plus water. Led by our platoon commander, Captain Thompson, and platoon sergeant, Keith, we followed a dirt road through the coastal scrub brush. The road narrowed to a trail, and before we were completely warmed up, we began to climb into the foothills. We hiked for fifty minutes then rested for ten, moving at a fifteen-minute-per-mile pace, hour after hour. In the first weeks we all struggled a bit. Some more than others—those new to the West Coast hills or those returning from deployment—but no one stopped. Everyone kept up or caught up by running. The trail wandered along a high ridgeline; on one side the Pacific Ocean could be seen through the haze of the morning marine layer, on the other we could catch glimpses of Range 130, where we would conduct our Close Quarter Battle Training in the months to come.

We were all seasoned Recon men and in great shape, but as the weeks and months of weekly twenty-plus-mile rucks went on, the hills made us hard and leaned us out. We went from gasping for air at the summit to laughing and joking the whole while, and the bonds between us strengthened through shared adversity.

One Thursday each month, we would run into a group of Marine recruits and their drill instructors completing the "Crucible": Marine Corps boot camp's defining seventy-two-hour field exercise that is designed to instill mental toughness. On the final morning of the Crucible, these recruits hiked to a high point from which the scrub had been cleared and a flagpole erected. There they would stop, drop their rucks, and in a ceremony raise the flag and receive their eagle, globe, and anchor, signifying the moment they became Marines.

We joked about it at the time, making comments about them not knowing what they were getting into, but I think the experience of hiking past newly minted Marines meant something for all of us. I know it did for me. They didn't know who we were, older Marines with longer hair in raggedy uniforms; but although most of us joined Recon to get away from "the regular Marine Corps," there exists in all of us the inextricable pride—usually hidden, often joked about, and sometimes denied—that being a Marine brings. These new Marines served as a reminder of what we were undertaking. We would be representing them, and all Marines, in SOCOM.

It was also a reminder of the saying, "brilliance in the basics." I still believe that there is no better measure of overall fitness than to carry a heavy load on your back over uneven terrain for long distances. It is self-paced suffering. Your shoulders, back, thighs, calves, and feet protest your continuing. Your fingers and arms grow numb; the skin on the balls of the feet and heels softens, turns white, and then blisters. But the blisters will eventually callus and harden and with them, your mind. And when you drop the ruck for a brief break at the top of a hill, you feel for a moment weightless, the light breeze against a sweat-soaked back bringing a shiver in even the hottest conditions, and for a moment the absence of the load makes the load worth it.

But there wasn't time to dwell on that then. We hiked and joked, and as weeks went by, we became faster and stronger and the hikes hurt less. We descended from the hills and crossed onto the beach. The last five-mile stretch was through the soft sand back to Camp Delmar. Keith began to implement team challenges when we reached the beach. We might find the massive tires from a military five-ton truck that we had to move back to camp, or a litter that required us to haul one of our teammates. Often, we returned to the obstacle course at Camp Del Mar and completed it five times before we could move back to the compound. This was stress inoculation at work. Doing hard things makes doing hard things easier. And when we reached the compound sometime around noon, we cleaned up and got started on the tasks for the day.

The message was clear: no one was going to congratulate you for getting to work. It was what you did when you got there that mattered.

CHAPTER 6

IT'S GOOD TO BE HARD

*We must remember that one man is much
the same as another, and that he is best
who is trained in the harshest school.*
—Thucydides

After I retired from the Marines in 2008, I almost immediately took up running ultramarathons. My son, Garrett, was now in high school, and he had started running cross-country, at least partially at my bidding. The first run we went on together, he was puffing to keep up after a mile. By the end of the month, he was leaving me in the dust on a three-mile run.

I've realized that as a father I tended to turn fun into work for my kids, and then get frustrated when they lost interest in whatever the activity was. I wanted to push them to be their best, but I only knew one way of doing that, the Marine Corps way. A pleasant hike in the coastal hills surrounding our house had to include map reading or survival training, and although one part of me could tell that I was going too far, I would usually continue to push until I sucked the fun out of the event.

Intent on developing a training plan to supplement Garrett's regular running practice, I went to a local bookstore and picked up a book on training for high school cross-country. While there I saw the book *Ultramarathon Man* by Dean Karnazes. I came home with both books.

It was the first time I had heard of ultra-distance races, which begin at fifty kilometers (thirty-one miles) and move to one hundred miles and beyond.

There are probably as many reasons that people join the military as there are service members. If you ask, patriotism usually tops the list, and I am sure that is a component of it. We also are just kids seeking approval, hoping to earn respect or a college degree, looking for a family, trying to escape one, or trying to feed one. But I would wager a paycheck that, whether it is admitted to or not, every man or woman who signs up is hoping to push beyond their perceived limits. And I would further wager that is a driving factor for those who make their way into special operations. For me, the Marines had been the only option, because it was the toughest, and toughest is the best.

Obsessively pursuing goals was a trait that had served me well in the Marines. I read *Ultramarathon Man* in a weekend, and never having run more than a half-marathon, signed up for a fifty-mile race, four months in the future. Now, serving as my own shrink, it is easy to see that I was looking for a challenge to fill the space left empty by retiring from the Marine Corps, and perhaps trying to prove to myself that I still had it. I was looking for purpose and found it in punishing my body. That had always been the measure of a man. How much can you take? How far can you go? Some fall in love with the adrenaline, leaping from airplanes, driving fast on motorcycles. I liked to shepherd that feeling, never wanting to become too comfortable with danger; I liked that fear kept me on edge. But I fell in love with the grind, with being comfortable in discomfort.

I had never particularly liked running while I was in the Marines. It was something we did a lot of, and I was pretty good at it, but I would seldom run more than necessary to ensure that I could do well on the semiannual three-mile fitness test. But now I was spending all day Saturdays on long runs of twenty miles or more.

That first fifty-miler sucked from about mile fifteen on. I started too fast, and my coastal North Carolina home left me unaccustomed to the hills and rugged, single-track trails of the Virginia mountains.

I finished, though, in a respectable time, and although I could barely walk for several days, I quickly signed up for another race.

I have since heard this called "Type 2" fun. While "Type 1" fun is something that is enjoyed while it is happening—a game with friends, a cookout, a concert, or a date—"Type 2" fun is an event that is not enjoyed until it is over, and even then, the enjoyment comes from having completed something hard.

But that is how I was brought up in the Marine Corps. Type 2 fun was all I knew. The team that completed the hardest patrol held the greatest bragging rights at the end, when we cleaned our gear, drank beer, and swapped stories. "Oh, you guys moved twelve miles? We moved fifteen and ran out of water on the last day."

And the Det was no different.

***

By July 2003, we had most of our weapons and equipment, and people could begin training in earnest. At this point we didn't know where our deployment would take us, but most of us expected Afghanistan. Our training followed a predictable pattern. Thursday hikes continued, and the team-competition aspect increased.

When we weren't in the field training, we spent our time refreshing skills. For medical training, the Docs (navy corpsmen) took the lead. We practiced giving each other IVs; treating sucking chest wounds with needle thoracentesis to relieve a collapsed lung; and nine-line medevac briefs. During weekly hikes, when we reached the beach we often found litters waiting with simulated casualties to be carried the final miles back to the compound.

Then came communications training. Refreshers on the radios: Satellite Communication (SATCOM), Very High Frequency (VHF), Ultrahigh Frequency (UHF), and the long-range communication workhorse, High Frequency (HF). HF radio waves bounce off the ionosphere and return to earth, so the strength and duration of the radio waves are aided by constructing antennas to best match the frequency being transmitted on. And so, armed with resistors and transistors and insulators and copper wire, we calculated and measured and built antennas to practice comm shots to distant stations.

Then we moved to our personal radio, the Multiband Inter/ Intra Team Radio, or MBITR. It was about the size of a brick, and it allowed us to communicate within close range over either the VHF or UHF band.

Next came a refresher on photography. While today we take for granted snapping a photo with our phones and instantly sharing it, transmitting photos securely over a radio was an ordeal. The photos were taken with a Canon digital single lens reflex (DSLR) camera and transferred to a hardened Panasonic Toughbook computer, where they were cleaned up, if needed, annotated in Photoshop, saved to a small file size, and transmitted over either HF or SATCOM. Depending on file size and strength of the connection, it often took minutes for each file to transmit. But, as the saying goes, a picture is worth a thousand words. The ability to send target photos simplified the mission of the recon team, allowing us to provide near-real-time information on activity on the objective.

For an assault team, knowing the specifics of the objective is critical for effective mission planning. Knowing the number, location, and type of entry points; the number and disposition of sentries; which areas are lit and which are in shadow—such details can add seconds to the element of surprise, and that saves lives.

Coates brought in an old friend, retired Marine and shooting instructor Pat Rogers, to run a refresher course in combat rifle and pistol marksmanship. Then we moved to the training areas of Camp Pendleton and rehearsed patrolling and reaction to contact. In elaborate scenarios, each team moved through the hills in full kit until a group of hidden targets popped into view. We engaged with live fire, seeking to quickly gain fire superiority. Then, since we were such a small team, we'd break contact in a series of well-rehearsed Immediate Action Drills. The scenarios required us to treat simulated casualties; request fire support from guns, ships, or fixed wing aircraft; call in a medevac bird; and move the team to a covered and concealed position from which to establish, mark, and secure a landing zone. Following each scenario, we held a team "hot wash," recalling the action, critiquing our performance, and pointing out areas for improvement. Then we hiked back to the staging area, dropped our gear, and waited to go again. We progressed from day to night and simulated aircraft fire to live bombs and guns. By the week's end, the plastic "Ivan" targets developed during the Cold War to represent the Russian hordes were more hole than target. After the final run-through for the final team, we packed up our gear and set out on a twenty-mile hike through the hills and canyons to get back home.

Most of us were friends already, but this training molded teams. I've mentioned Sid who served as my Assistant Team Leader. Mike was our point man. Absolutely reliable. His hair prematurely gray, he could be counted on to make thoughtful decisions in crisis. Ben and Bo had recently returned from a deployment for the initial invasion of Iraq to join the team. Mike, Ben, and Bo had worked together before, but I knew them only through reputation and observation during their training. Ben was smarter than all of us, with a quick wit and love of literature. Bo was our communicator, a mountain of a man who understood the mysteries of radio waves and how they interacted with the ionosphere. Eric was tall and lanky, a mechanic at First Force Recon before he took the Indoc. Although frequently abrasive, he was a workhorse. And Doc Arnold was competent and quiet. He always looked like he was not having fun, but rarely complained. I'm sure the other team leaders felt they had the best teams, as they should have; but I knew that I did. I recognized every day that I was fortunate to lead these men, and tried every day to be up to the task.

We learned to suffer in silence by watching those who led us. Because we didn't allow weakness or hesitation or fear, I always felt I was the only one who felt it. I've since heard it called "impostor syndrome," the feeling that at any moment the qualified in the room are going to realize that you don't belong and should never have been there. But somehow this feeling was able to exist alongside extreme cockiness—or perhaps I did such a good job of masking fear with bravado that I was often able to fool myself. But the cockiness was justified, because I knew that for any of my failings, as a team we were capable of anything.

One of the first pieces of guidance I gave out was that, as a team, we would take on any mission we could get. No mission was too small or unimportant. We adopted the unofficial motto, "We do windows." And as our training progressed, I volunteered us for the odd, the unusual, the less desired. Any mission that would give us a chance to show Colonel Coates what we were capable of.

It is a military axiom that time spent on reconnaissance is seldom wasted. Before conducting a raid or assault on an objective, you need people on the ground to get "eyes-on." A Reconnaissance and Surveillance (R&S) team inserts to observe what is happening on the target and report back critical information, to allow the assault force to plan:

> What is the size and layout of the building?

> What is the pattern of life in the surrounding area?

> How is the building guarded, and what is the security posture?

> How many enemy forces are present, and how are they armed?

> Is the person(s) we are looking for there?

> What entry points should be used, and what types of explosive charges will be needed to gain entry?

The list goes on.

While today's advances in satellite imagery and the ubiquitousness of drones can answer many of these questions, there will always be questions that can be answered only by someone "on target." An R&S team also can remain to support the raid, providing precision fire (snipers) in support of the assault force; assisting with isolation—keeping more bad guys from showing up; and helping with containment—keeping bad guys from getting away.

To retain the element of surprise, the reconnaissance team might insert via parachute, subsurface (dive), or helicopter. But in almost all cases, the final leg to the objective consists of a long foot movement with heavy loads, followed by days and nights of tedium—lying out in the weather or in an abandoned building, observing and reporting on the target while trying to maintain your own security and safety.

Then, after receiving last-minute updates, the assault force climbs onto helicopters, flies in, hits the target, flies back, and gets the glory. Meanwhile the recon team returns to debrief, clean weapons and equipment, and dump MRE bags full of their own excrement (you don't want to know) before taking a shower and hitting the rack.

We volunteered for R&S every time. Taking the shit job and doing it well had been the recipe for whatever success I had accumulated up to this point, and I saw no reason to change it up now.

***

Coates managed to borrow Jon Laplume from Natick Labs on a semi-permanent basis to build and buy our equipment suite, and now equipment was beginning to arrive. The road to our small compound was a traffic jam, with FedEx trucks unloading all the items needed to organize and outfit a special operations unit.

We paid a local company to recreate the venerable ALICE pack— large, in desert tan, with added pockets sewn on. The acronym was a throwback to the 1970s, when All-Purpose Lightweight Individual Carrying Equipment referred to an entire complement of load-bearing accessories, but now had become synonymous with the sixty-two-liter workhorse. The ALICE pack first saw use in Vietnam, and while the Marine Corps had moved away from it for more modern designs, the rugged, external-frame pack was capable of being loaded to bursting with all the items needed on a week-long recon patrol. When you added in the load-bearing vest and everything stuffed in pockets, plus weapon, the loads frequently topped 120 pounds.

We referred to equipment we carried by line number.

Line 1 equipment included the weapon, uniform, and pocket items. This was the bare minimum needed to sustain you for a short period of time. The chest pockets of our camouflage uniforms held a compass; a survival mirror; a small notebook called a patrol log, with a pencil for noting anything of intel value; and an MRE spoon. Everything was connected by lengths of parachute cord. These "dummy cords" prevented loss by exhausted men. There were tubes of camouflage paint for darkening faces, which needed to be reapplied frequently. Large cargo pockets held a laminated map and alcohol pens, a cloth neon air panel, and almost always a can of Copenhagen. Blood chits (a notice written in multiple languages, promising reward for assistance provided), survival maps, survival money, a toothbrush with the handle cut down (because ounces make pounds), and a travel toothpaste. We wore Leatherman tools on thick belts that could be used to rappel in a pinch.

We carried M4 carbines with a magazine inserted. An Aimpoint sight mounted on the top rail and an AN/PEQ-2 infrared laser on the side, activated with a push button. Sound suppressors added length and weight but reduced noise and flash. Flashlights were used for assaults but were usually removed for reconnaissance.

I carried one of the team's two M203 grenade launchers attached beneath my rifle barrel. That responsibility came with an additional mesh vest (included in Line 2), with pockets to hold twenty 40 mm shells, (sixteen high-explosive shells and four of the longer illumination rounds).

Eric carried the Squad Automatic Weapon (SAW) with an ELCAN optic mounted on the feed-tray rail. The SAW was equipped with a shortened SOF-variant barrel that reduced weight but allowed the weapon to quickly overheat, increasing the potential for "cook offs," when the heat causes the weapon to continue firing after the trigger is released. Also known as a "runaway gun."

Line 2 is the load-bearing vest (LBV). The form factor has changed over the years, from a "Y" harness to an "H" harness to a chest rig, but the job of the LBV is to carry ammo and survival items. Twelve spare magazines loaded with twenty-eight rounds each, mixed with tracer and ball; four quarts of water; a butt pack stuffed to the gills with a survival kit, IV fluid kit, emergency chow, a survival blanket, and a larger air panel called a VS-17. On the straps, infrared strobe lights were attached, probably another knife, a smoke grenade, and room for frags. In training, we carried blue practice grenades for the weight and taped the pin rings down so they wouldn't catch on anything. Everyone carried an MBITR radio and at least one spare battery. Line 2 is never removed unless adding or removing warming layers. You learned to adjust it to a position that allowed for something approximating sleep.

Line 3 items were carried in the ruck. Light stuff went in the bottom to keep the load up high. Sleeping kit consisted of a Ranger roll: a rubber poncho and thin poncho-liner combo. There usually wasn't room for sleeping bags—we followed the mantra, travel light/freeze at night.

A spare pair of socks, extra warming layers, the Gore-Tex jacket and pants, which were great in rain and blocked wind, but were noisy to move in.

We ate Meals, Ready-To-Eat (MREs), shelf-stable food from of plastic bags. These meals were "field-stripped" to reduce excess weight, all extra packaging and unnecessary items left behind. The single spoon, dummy-corded to my pocket, was used to eat. We usually limited ourselves to one MRE per day to save weight and space. Each meal was roughly 1250 calories. Not a lot for grown men moving miles under enormous loads. It was a large part of the reason we all had visible abs.

Batteries—there were always batteries to be carried: AAs, AAAs, DL 123s, and the big, heavy BA 5590s used by our radios. Random objects required their own batteries—button batteries for the Aimpoint, C batteries for the Simrad KN200F sniper night sight.

There were extra boxes of ammo for the Squad Automatic Weapon, pole-less litters, additional medical gear, binoculars, spotting scopes, camera and lenses, more batteries, tripod, Toughbook computer, cables to connect it all, cleaning kit for our rifles, for the camera. Brushes and pencil erasers to clean connections for the radio's. Then there were the radios themselves to cover the UHF, VHF, HF, and SATCOMM spectrums, the antennas that come with the radio, then a FEAK—field expedient antenna kit. Communications logs, called yellow canaries for the color of the pages, and cryptographic security items.

More batteries, more smoke grenades, Claymore mines for perimeter defense, thermite grenades for destroying our classified equipment if capture was imminent. Pop-up flares for signaling, and at least another four quarts of water carried in two-liter canteens, or a CamelBak. Then there were the small items that had saved your ass too many times to leave behind, stuffed wherever there was room: 550 cord, a lighter, hot sauce, baby wipes, Mrs. Dash, beef jerky, and Ziploc bags covered in green military duct tape, to keep things dry.

Some equipment was mission-dependent: ropes, carabiners, climbing protection, climbing harness, SPIE (Special Patrol Insertion/Extraction) harness, chemlights, sniper rifles and ammo, blocks of C-4 explosives, det cord, blasting caps, M-60 fuse ignitors.

And then we carried duplicates of everything because we lived by the mantra, "two is one and one is none."

There was little room for personal items or personal baggage, but some were superstitious and carried religious items—a crucifix or a symbol of one of the many patron saints of those who go into harm's way: Saint Michael the Archangel (patron saint of the paratroopers) and Saint Barbara (patron saint of the Marines); Saint Christopher, the patron saint of travelers; or Saint Brendan, the patron saint of mariners. One guy wore what he called his "honcho necklace," with a Buddha, a cross, a Star of David, and a crescent, just to keep his bases covered. One dog tag was worn around the neck and the other attached to a boot eyelet, to aid in the identification of loose limbs. Although I never did, many Recon Marines got a "meat tag" tattoo on the torso under the arm, with their dog tag information: name, blood type, and religion.

With the things we carried came the things we destroyed: ankles, knees, hips, shoulders, livers, and frequently, long-term relationships. While the life caused many marriages to end quickly, damage to the body was insidious and slow in its onset, kept at bay because we needed to continue to operate. And because we seldom associated with those outside of Recon, we failed to find it odd that thirty-something-year-old men limped and hobbled and ached and cracked. Otherwise-healthy young men complained about torn labrums, ACL damage, bursitis, patellar tendinitis, and plantar fasciitis. Stress fractures were common and often self-misdiagnosed as simply shin splints. When I completed my retirement physical, the doctor, after taking an x-ray, asked how many times I had broken my leg. I replied, "never." He laughed and slid the x-ray into the lightboard and turned it on. "Your tibia looks like a piece of bamboo." Multiple thick rings circled the bone where stress fractures had healed. But they never stopped me from going on patrol.

If ignored long enough, a nagging pain simply becomes the cost of doing business. Then, after you retire, you discover that vitamin M (500 mg Motrin) should not be chewed for breakfast. Then you realize that a forty-year-old should be able to descend a staircase without turning sideways and keeping a death grip on the railing, or that rising from bed shouldn't require mental preparation.

I haven't run an ultramarathon since COVID-19 shut things down, but swear I'll get back to it. Just to prove that I can. While I have grown and matured in the years since I retired, there is still a strong pull of the rules we lived by: two is one and one is none; you can't use what you don't have; compromise is mission failure; if it can go wrong—it will; when all else fails, resort to unrelenting violence; and if you aren't living on the edge, you're taking up too much room.

CHAPTER 7
IT'S HARD TO BE SMART

*Combat is fast, unfair, cruel, and dirty. It is meant
to be that way so that the terrible experience is
branded into the memory of those who are fortunate
enough to survive. It is up to those survivors to
ensure that the experience is recorded and passed
along to those who just might want to try it.*
—Bruce H. Norton, *Force Recon Diary,* 1969.

Most of us previously had received mountain training at the Marine
Corps Mountain Warfare Training Center at Pickel Meadows,
California, near Bridgeport. But I had not completed the Marines
Corps' famous Summer or Winter Mountain Leaders Courses, which
train students to lead a unit in mountain combat. The summer course
teaches climbing, mountain movement, navigation, and weather reading, and the winter course focuses on winter survival, cross-country and telemark skiing, and ice climbing. A few of our number had
previously served as Bridgeport instructors. Red, Chunks, and Major
Craig Kozeniesky were highly experienced in this environment and led
the training.

After our return from Iraq, we spent a lot of time in the mountains of Bridgeport, California training for what we hoped would be a deployment to Afghanistan.

In late September, 2003 we culminated our patrolling training in the peaks of Bridgeport. We established ourselves at the base camp and started each morning with huge breakfast in the base camp chow hall, then hiked to the training areas. At base camp I hadn't felt much difference, but at nearly seven thousand feet the air was thinner, and it took more energy to accomplish the same work. At the training areas, we climbed all day, practicing lead climbing, setting routes, and follow climbing. At the end of each day, we changed into PT gear and ran miles back to Pickel Meadows. Now, we could really feel the elevation, like sucking air through a straw. The trick was to slow the pace and slow the breathing. As we descended, the difference was measurable, the air became richer and breathing came easier.

Each day, the instructors set up lanes and we split among them, waiting to climb or serve as safety and belay. On the final day of climbing, I had completed several lanes when the Yoyo Lane freed up, just as Chunks yelled out, "Hey, finish the lane you're on and let's break for lunch."

"Screw it, I'm going to hit this one." I turned to Sid. "Belay me?"

"You got it."

The purpose of the Yoyo Lane was to simulate a lead climb up a concave pitch at the edge of our abilities. If we couldn't make it and fell, we would be belayed to the ground. If we did make it to the top, we were to let go and, again, be lowered to the ground thirty feet below.

Sid took up the rope. The climb was classified as a 5.6, a relatively challenging pitch that ran roughly thirty feet up a crevice in the rock face. I focused on maintaining three points of contact, finding nubs of rock that my thick military boots could grip, and using my leg strength to the greatest degree possible. I made my way up slowly, testing handholds and footholds as I rose, reaching back to pull carabiners from my climbing harness, attaching them to protection in the wall, and clipping my rope into it. When lead climbing, the requirement for focus is absolute. Hips over feet, three points of contact, conserve energy in the arms whenever possible, focus always on thinking, "What is the next best move I can make?"

Near the top, the toehold of my left foot was slipping. I turned my hips, pressed harder into the rock to steady myself, and found a crevice above my head to jam my fingers into. Stable, I was able to move to a better foothold and make it to the top of the climb. At the top, I looked back over my shoulder to make sure Sid was ready, then released my grip on the rock.

It takes about 1.2 seconds for a 180-pound man to fall thirty feet. For the first 0.2 seconds I thought nothing of it; for the next half second I thought, "Man, I'm falling fast." Finally, at about 0.8 seconds, I yelled, "Falling!" The signal to be belayed. Then I hit the ground, instinctively landing in a parachute-landing fall (PLF), contacting the balls of my feet, then collapsing to my side to absorb the impact, spreading the force over the calf, thigh, buttocks, and pushup muscle. This saved me from serious damage; but my left ankle caught between two rocks, held immobile as the rest of me rolled onto my side. A branding iron of pain stabbed me.

Sid was there apologizing. He screwed up the belay by not taking in enough slack. The docs were on me, checking me over, then helping me back down to the level ground and into a safety vehicle. X-rays revealed that nothing was broken, but ligaments had been torn. At the MWTC clinic, I was given a boot cast to wear and told to stay off my feet for the remainder of the trip.

The rest of the guys finished climbing, then began planning for the patrol that was to be the main test—a multiday movement over multiple twelve-thousand-foot peaks. I was crushed not to be able to go, so I threw myself into helping with preparations. Sid would lead the team. It was the first time I had ever missed a patrol with my guys, and it felt shitty.

The morning that the guys stepped off on their patrol, I learned that some of our support guys were going to be taking a mule-packing class from a Bridgeport instructor. Mules are still used to ferry equipment in the mountains and are often the only way to deliver heavy loads deep into the backcountry. Since we were still anticipating going to Afghanistan, this seemed like a valuable skill, and so I joined them. For two days, we learned to attach painters to mules and build and lash loads to the amazing animals. After our training, we put what we had learned to the test by packing the mules with food and water and moving to locations along the team's routes to emplace resupply caches.

With no one back from the patrol to tell me not to go, I decided that it would be a good idea for me to tag along. I could ride a mule most of the time, so I wouldn't have to worry about walking. I could not wear the boot cast and get my foot into the stirrup, so I taped up my still-ugly, swollen ankle and shoved it back into a regular boot. We spent a couple of days moving to predetermined locations to drop off our caches of MREs and water cans. It was wonderful time, riding slowly through the eastern slope of the Sierra Mountains among the junipers, buckthorn, willow, and pinyon pine. The mules were surefooted and, as their reputation holds, sometimes stubborn, which I think had to do more with them knowing their capabilities. They would get you where you wanted to go, but would take their own route and their own time to get there. I was often terrified as my mule clomped along a thread of a trail on the side slope of a mountain, but I really couldn't walk, so dismounting wasn't much of an option.

When the teams made it back to base camp, they were weary from the exertion, but there was the usual pride in having done the difficult thing, the jokes of how cold it had been, and the competition to determine whose route had been the most difficult. I hated the feeling of being on the outside of that. It was a place I had never found myself before, and I vowed never to be there again.

After returning from Bridgeport, we began planning for a raid on a location in the high desert. I found an ankle brace that allowed me to walk and a boot I could wear it under, and I volunteered for the reconnaissance.

Finally, the focus of our training turned to Close Quarters Battle (CQB). In a traditional Force Recon training cycle, CQB training came close to deployment. That is because of the level of shooting speed and accuracy demanded in order to be qualified to conduct In-extremis Hostage Rescue (IHR) and other direct action (DA) missions, and the perishability of the skill.

The focus was on close-in marksmanship: one hundred yards and in with the rifle, and fifty yards and in with the pistol. We all had been through this training multiple times, but now the tolerances were tightened, greater accuracy expected, greater speed demanded. Head shots from the holster in a second and a half. Shooting while moving, shooting at night with pistol and rifle lights, shooting with gas masks and wearing night-vision goggles.

We returned time and again to transition drills. If the rifle trigger is pressed and it doesn't fire, the action is instinctual: release the firing grip and move the dominant hand to the pistol, breaking the retention device and establishing a good fighting grip, simultaneously with the support hand guiding the rifle to the opposite hip, out of the way. The dominant hand draws the pistol, and both hands meet in a solid grip, punching the weapon toward the target, releasing the safety, and firing a shot into a rectangle the size of a 3x5 card. All of this needed to happen in under one and one-half seconds.

At this point, USSOCOM gave us our deployment order. We were headed to Iraq, not Afghanistan, and would be designated Task Unit (TU) Raider, named for our WWII forefathers. It was a title we were honored to carry, and a lineage that the surviving Raiders were thrilled to see continue. We would work for the commander of a Naval Special Warfare Task Group from SEAL Team One. Our primary mission would be targeting former regime element (FRE) members and terrorist cell leaders. The FRE had been a part of Saddam's inner circle, many immortalized in the "Iraq's most wanted" deck of playing cards. They were now working against coalition efforts to stabilize Iraq and allow for free elections.

After weeks of working on the range, we moved into the shoot houses and our training took on an added sense of urgency. We progressed from two-man clears of adjoining rooms to nighttime, multistory, multi-breach-point clears with the entire platoon, with rooms holding both shoot and no-shoot targets.

Missing the kill zone on a shoot target more than once carried the possibility of dismissal. Shooting a no-shoot target meant a trip in full kit to the top of the massive "Hostage Hill" that loomed behind the shoot house. At the top, red-faced and panting, you were to inscribe your name on the giant white cross that represented the innocents killed by your carelessness. You only got one trip up the hill. I had made mine years before and vowed never to let it happen again. You quickly learn that speed is fine but accuracy is final.

We cleared rooms in a seemingly chaotic but prescribed fashion. First, we tossed in a flash-bang grenade. The noise, flash, and smoke disoriented anyone inside and bought us a split-second advantage. The number-one man followed the bang, engaging any immediate threats in the doorway, then taking care of any targets in his sector of responsibility. The number-two man was on his heels, clearing in the opposite direction. Their sectors of fire overlapped in the center of the room.

If there were people in the room, we looked at the hands. The targets used in training came with objects ranging from beer bottles to cell phones to hair dryers, to machetes, to submachine guns. We had to identify and engage only threat targets. Non-threats were controlled initially with verbiage, then physically restrained. The mantra was: control the room, control the living, control the dead.

We quickly searched the room for anyone hiding, then marked it with a small chemical light stick and moved on. If we had detainees, they were shepherded to a marshalling area near the entry point, where they were separated into groups: Hostages, Unknowns, and Tangos (terrorists). With multiple teams, the house was usually clear in just a few minutes. The radio call "last room" indicated that the limits of the structure had been reached and the building was clear. Then we turned to processing the house: conducting a detailed search of each room and looking for items of intelligence value, evidence, weapons, bomb-making material, and so on. Finally, we radioed a HUTS report to higher, identifying the number and status of (if applicable) Hostages, Unknowns, Tangos, and Shooters. We were seldom on the target for more than thirty minutes, reducing the opportunity for reinforcements to arrive.

With a better understanding of how we would be employed, we decided to restructure into smaller assault teams. Sid was the next-senior guy, so I lost him. He became the leader of team five; and because Ben was so adept at comm, I let Sid take Bo, who had been our communicator. I hated to lose them, but while it is tough, I believe that if you give up someone and that doesn't hurt, then they are not the right person. Jack was given team six and filled it out with guys from the other teams.

In December, 2003 we flew to Mercury, Nevada, a former Cold War nuclear test site, for our final set of full mission-profile rehearsal exercises. Between 1951 and the early 1990s, over one thousand nuclear weapons were tested on over thirteen hundred square miles of high desert plains and rugged mountains. Large swaths of the facility were still off-limits, due to radiation.

This was an opportunity to work out the capabilities of the entire detachment. The logistics folks coordinated the transportation, set up the camp, and provided the support necessary to feed, water, and sustain a small town's worth of Marines, far from any resources. The Intelligence section—under Major Jerry Carter and the intel chief, Bret—established connections to secure databases and pored over imagery, uniting the collective power of the various "INTS" (intelligence disciplines): SIGINT (signals intelligence), HUMINT (human Intelligence), and GEOINT (geospatial intelligence). Together, they were able to pinpoint the enemy location, a small cluster of buildings located deep in the mountains.

As promised, I volunteered team four for reconnaissance, but rather than moving on foot, we would be vehicle-mounted, using the G-Wagon IFAVs (interim fast attack vehicles). My five-man team was able to stuff into two vehicles all our equipment, and enough fuel and water and camouflage nets to hide the vehicles during the day.

After mission-planning, inspections, and rehearsals, we carefully backed our IFAVs into the waiting CH-53 helicopters. We inserted at night, and to avoid compromise they set us down well out of sight or sound of the target. The crew chiefs manned machine guns in the doors and kept up a steady conversation with the pilot, passing him vital information about our height above ground and hidden obstacles. The helo shuddered and sank until gravity won out and the wheels slammed to the ground. We scurried to free the ratchet straps holding us in the aircraft, gunned the engines, drove far enough away to escape the dust storm kicked up by the helicopter, then stopped and took up security positions. In the blackness, the swirling sand made the rotor tips glow green and cut circles in the midnight sky, a phenomenon called the Kopp-Etchells effect.

After the helicopter lifted off into the sky and disappeared, we shut down the engines and conducted SLLS—or Stop, Look, Listen, Smell—just as we would on a foot patrol, to focus on any indication that our insertion had been observed, and to allow our senses to become attuned to the environment. After several minutes, I was satisfied that we had inserted unseen. I gave the signal to start the engines, and we pulled out, following our compass heading.

We picked our way through the desert in the night to a concealed position two thousand meters from the enemy camp. It was a fenced-in compound with a series of buildings ostensibly being used to construct bombs, manned by role players who followed a schedule of coming and going, security patrols, and shift changes. It was up to us to determine the pattern of life in the camp and relay that information back to our Combat Operations Center (COC), to allow them to develop the best plan.

The December night was bitter-cold. When the sky grew pink enough for me to make out the small pocket thermometer I carried, it read five degrees. Our canteens were ice blocks. We lugged the five-gallon water cans to a position to catch the first rays of sunlight, in hope of thawing them enough for water by noon.

After taking care of our work priorities, Mike and I needed to move forward to pinpoint the target. I gave Ben a five-point contingency plan, called a GOTWA:

Going (where we are)
Others I'm taking with me
Time I plan to be gone
What to do if I don't return
Actions on enemy contact (for both me and them)

With that, Mike and I crept forward through the wadis and scrub brush to a point on a small rise where we could observe the camp. Mike took photos and I counted men. We would send in a SALUTE report detailing the enemy's Size, Activity, Location, Uniform, Time and date, and Equipment. We then began detailed reporting of anything the assault team would need to know. We took a panorama of photographs to send back via satellite, to be printed, stitched together, and pored over by the assault teams.

The camp was surrounded by a tall, razor-wire-topped, chain-link fence with a gate on its east end. Three structures were spread out within the compound. Two were small storage buildings, and the other was the nerve center of the operation. We sent back diagrams with distances between buildings, and fence heights. These were determined by using the milliradian scale in our scopes. That required maintaining a list of the known heights, in yards, of certain standard objects, then punching a rudimentary equation into our solar-powered calculators: height of the target in yards multiplied by one thousand, then dividing the resulting number by the height of the object in milliradians. Each of the small "Mil dots" in our scopes represented one-640th of a circle.

We catalogued the guards and assigned them nicknames based on identifiable features. They became known as Bean Pole, Droopy Drawers, or Mustache Guy. A guard force of six men manned the compound, with vehicles arriving at irregular intervals to deliver or remove items or conduct inspections.

We tried to establish pattern of life: guard shift changes, inspections, periods of increased activity, and times when there was a lull. Do they conduct "Stand To," heightened security at dusk and dawn? During the Revolutionary War, Robert Rogers, the founder of the Rangers, noted that these were the times the French and Indians attacked, and he insisted that everyone be awake and alert. Stand To is a practice that is still observed, and it is a good indication of a disciplined unit.

After nearly twenty-four hours of "eyes on," and just before dark, the role players manning the objective gathered and were accounted for. The sentry positions were replaced with mannequin targets in the guard tower and at the gate. Heavy bullet traps were moved into position inside the buildings to absorb rounds, and mannequins were placed in front of them.

That night we met up with the assault force and guided them to a release point. Mike and I led the support-by-fire position to the location we had observed from. The snipers selected their positions, and gunners set up medium machine guns on tripods, while the assault force maneuvered around to breach the fence and make entry. On the coordinated signal, our snipers dropped the visible sentries; then the machine guns opened up, eliminating targets in the open and then shifting fires to allow the assault force to breach the gate. On the breach, the machine guns silenced. Through night vision I could make out two-man teams clearing the out-buildings and checking the dead. Then came the thump of a breaching charge on the main building, and a flood of assaulters swarming through the opening.

Suddenly, over comms from aircraft we got a report of reinforcements heading up a dirt road toward our position. Our Joint Terminal Air Controller (JTAC) calmly spoke to the waiting gunships and brought in a gun run from a Cobra helicopter onto a line of junk vehicles in a draw several kilometers away. The reinforcements were neutralized.

After our training in Mercury, then a brief Christmas break, it was a flurry of pre-deployment activity. We conducted a joint exercise with the SEALs, involving a number of joint D.A. missions and staff interoperability work. They were amazed by the robust intel and fires capability we brought. They recognized then that, once deployed, our assets would be their assets. A fact that would cause friction later.

After all the preparation was done, we were given two weeks of leave. Tracy had planned a family road trip. In March 2004 we drove up the coast, stopping at points of interest: the Winchester House; Hearst Castle in San Simeon; Monterey; and San Francisco, where for several days we hiked through Chinatown and visited Alcatraz. On the drive home we hit Disneyland. During times like this I felt I was trying to pack a week of fun and fatherhood into each day. And while we had a blast, I kept finding my mind wandering to preparations that still needed to be made, or items that we needed to rehearse, or scenarios to plan for.

Once back at Camp Pendleton, we packed up and prepared to depart. The headquarters and staff flew out on the first wave to get in-country and begin preparations. The teams were scheduled to be on the final flight. When the morning came for our flight, I packed up, kissed Tracy and the kids goodbye, and went to the airfield—only to find that the plane was broken.

We repeated this the next day…and the next…and the next. At one point, Kallie, who was seven at the time, came to me crying, begging me to tell my boss that I was sick and couldn't go to war. But after days of the same routine, Garrett and Kallie were beginning to believe that I wasn't actually leaving. It became both easier and harder each day to say goodbye. Easier, because it seemed as though I would never leave, and harder, because it was like playing Russian roulette. If you keep pulling the trigger, eventually you will hit the loaded cylinder. Finally, after almost a week, when the kids came home from school and Tracy from work, I wasn't there—and wouldn't be for the next two hundred and ten days, or so.

On 16 April we arrived at the airfield to be waved aboard the massive C-17 Globemaster, and we lifted off for Baghdad.

CHAPTER 8

SPEED IS FINE,
ACCURACY IS FINAL

We are what we repeatedly do. Excellence,
then, is not an act, but a habit.
—Will Durant

We stepped off the plane at the Baghdad International Airport (BIAP) in the middle of the night on April 18 2004. Landing at night had the desired effect of making the massive aircraft a more difficult target for rocket-propelled grenades (RPGs). The night air was an oven without a trace of moisture. Waves of heat rose from the tarmac. The guys who had arrived before us rushed around to unload bags and pack them into waiting vehicles. Forklift drivers raced each to other grab pallets and swing them onto flatbed trucks. My memory is a little hazy due to jet lag and a brief layover in Rota, Spain, where we worked to throw back as many beers as possible before last call. We loaded up and were driven to our corner of the BIAP compound through various checkpoints manned by national guard soldiers. When we arrived, we were pointed toward cots set up three men to a room. Welcome to Iraq.

We were in the Radwaniyah Palace complex, or RPC. At the top of the hill sat Saddam's Radwaniyah Palace, which had been claimed by the Fifth Special Forces Group during the initial invasion. It now housed the rotating teams from Fifth Group, as well as the headquarters for all special operations in the Arabian Peninsula, of which we were a part. It was called the Combined Joint Special Operations Task Force–Arabian Peninsula, or CJSOTF-AP, for short.

Down the hill from the palace stood a multi-story building built of pink marble. Saddam had used it to accommodate overflow guests, or those he didn't want too close. Across the road from that, close to the compound's high, razor-wire-topped wall, sat a series of low-slung, earth-colored structures designed to blend into the scenery. These had been the servants' quarters. They were where we lived. I wondered if our meager accommodations were chosen to send some type of oblique message, since we were the new guys on the block, but I didn't have the time to give it too much thought, Plus, we didn't have to climb stairs with our equipment, so I chose to look on the bright side.

I roomed with Mike and Eric. Our space was large enough to hold our cots and most of our equipment. In the wide hallway outside of our room, we each set extra cots to stage our assault gear, which consisted of a pistol belt, bullet bouncer, helmet, NODs (night optic devices), gas mask and chemical-protective suits (in case of chem-bio weapons), and my breaching shotgun. Our weapons stayed with us on the compound most of the time. I always carried at least my pistol. I had brought a shoulder holster with me that was great for running or going to the gym.

The hallways of the building extended out like spokes from a large common room in front, where we maintained a small supply of ammunition and the consumable materials we would need to replenish after a mission: chemlights, flex cuffs, latex gloves, and Ziploc bags. It was also where we held platoon meetings. One side of the room was covered with wrestling mats, and most evenings would find several of us training in jujitsu. Later, we chipped in to purchase a satellite dish and television, and we mounted it there. We'd gather between missions to watch Lance Armstrong win his sixth Tour de France (we didn't yet know that he was doping) and the 2004 Athens Olympics.

Across the road, set back in a grove of palm trees and with a newly refurbished swimming pool behind it, was the task group headquarters and Joint Operations Center (JOC) from NSW Squadron One, under whose control we would be operating.

Now that we were all here, we started the RIP/TOA process. This is the Relief in Place/ Turnover of Authority between an incoming unit and the outgoing one. The only problem was that, technically, there was not an outgoing unit. There had not been a task unit (TU) based in Baghdad before us, so our turnover was conducted by SEAL Lieutenant Jocko Willink. I had worked with Jocko years before, when he was an enlisted SEAL and we deployed together, so it was great to see him again. Jocko would later return to lead TU Bruiser through the fight in Ramadi.

He filled us in on the situation on the ground and gave us the only real leads that we had to work with: two unnamed terrorist cell leaders who had been dubbed "X" and "Z." All that was known about them was that they existed. Each was represented on the JOC targeting board by a shadowy silhouette at the top of a hierarchy of other silhouettes. A line and block chart that meant nothing more than there were bad guys doing bad things, and the only thing we knew for certain was that the bad things kept happening and would continue to happen until we stopped them.

We left the target-finding to Major Carter, Bret, and their intel guys. They dug through intel reports and spoke with connections. We learned that our task group (TG) commander and navy boss, Commander Bill Wilson, was going to split up our intelligence section and parcel them out among the SEAL TUs spread throughout the country. Some of our counterintelligence, signals intelligence, and intel fusion specialists were sent to Northern Iraq, some to Al-Anbar Province, and one of our counterintelligence Marines was sent to work in the Green Zone—the secure area in downtown Baghdad from where the nominal Iraq government was being run—as a liaison between the TG and other agencies. While these moves forced us to shift from the model we had trained for, ultimately it was a massively beneficial decision. By spreading our guys out across Iraq, we gained access to mountains of intelligence, from which these truly amazing individuals were able to piece together what may have been the most comprehensive intelligence picture in Iraq at the time.

As a part of the memorandum of agreement between the Marine Corps and Naval Special Warfare, Colonel Coates agreed to step aside, because he outranked Commander Bill Wilson, the TG commander (a navy commander is the equivalent of a Marine lieutenant colonel). Although he was still our commanding officer, day-to-day operations for TU Raider were run by Major Kozeniesky, and our senior enlisted leader, Ripper. Coates was ordered to report to Fallujah, where he was assigned by the I Marine Expeditionary Force commander, Lieutenant General James Conway, to serve as the "point man" for the Fallujah Brigade, an all-Iraqi force. He was the right man for the job, considering the experience he had gained as a young captain in El Salvador overseeing counterinsurgency efforts.

The patch worn on the shoulder of our World War II Raider forefathers featured a dark blue pentagonal shield with a red diamond, surrounded by the stars of the Southern Cross constellation. This template served as the model for all First Marine Division units in the Pacific campaign during WWII. The Raiders insignia was distinctive because within the red diamond sat a smiling skull. The insignia was worn with pride by Raiders, admired and envied by other Marines, and feared by the enemy. By the time we arrived in Iraq, a hand-painted sign featuring the emblem marked our camp. The compound itself was named Camp Myler, for Sergeant Christian Myler. Christian was one of the Marines selected to serve in the detachment who tragically passed away in motorcycle accident shortly after we formed.

The other TU stationed aboard BIAP was a NATO SOF unit from Poland's Grupa Reagowina Operacyjno Mobilnego—or Operational Mobile Response Group. They were better known as the GROM, which in Polish means "thunder," so they were named TU Thunder. It was my first time working with them, but they held true to their reputation of being incredibly skilled professionals. Most were massive, bearded men well over six feet. Not the sort of guys you want coming after you in the night. The exception was the TU Thunder's lone female operator, Kate. Kate was fit, unassuming, and thankfully unbearded, but as one of the unit's snipers she was among the most lethal.

We quickly fell into a routine: get up, wander across the street to eat, head out to the range just down the road for a quick warm-up with the rifle and pistol, then out to train or work on refining SOPs. Upon our return, I'd poke my head in the JOC to see if anything was shaking, eat lunch, work on equipment or vehicles, then PT late in the evening when the sun went down. We ran circles around the compound, on roads that had once housed Saddam and his guests. Saddam was fond of wild animals and kept them in cages. Many of them were freed during the initial invasion, and there were rumors that a lion still lurked in the wooded areas, but no one ever saw it. We did encounter one near the Green Zone, a lion kept caged and tended to by an army unit.

I had been given the task of developing our vehicle SOPs. We had recognized that the G-Wagons were not going to be adequate for transporting loaded assault teams, so before we left, our mechanics managed to scrounge some barely serviceable Humvees. These were shipped over with us, and the mechs transformed an old storage building into what we dubbed the "monster garage." From the building came hammering, sparks, curses, and grunts, but what eventually emerged were rebuilt assault vehicles. Yes, they looked a little Frankenstein-like, with scrap steel bolted on as armor, and metal fenceposts used to form wire cutters—or anti-decapitation devices, as they are known. These prevented wire that was strung across a road from beheading the vehicle gunner, who manned the roof-mounted machine gun. Our communications guys installed radios and devices designed to block the signal from radio-controlled improvised explosive devices (RC-IEDs).

The armorers procured pintle mounts and attached them to every door, and each vehicle carried a mix of light, medium, and heavy machine guns. Then I had Team Four load up, and we set out to a small, abandoned housing area near the compound to develop the vehicle tactics we would use.

If we were to be assaulting from our vehicles, we had two options: the "soft hit," where we stopped the vehicles some distance away and allowed the assault teams to approach on foot to retain surprise; or the "hard hit," in which, as the name implies, we come in hard and fast, relying on speed and violence of action.

Using the abandoned neighborhood, we rehearsed options: how and where to position vehicles, how to best unload the assaulters, techniques for isolating and containing the area by observation and by fire.

We rigged hooks on the sides of the Humvees to carry ladders that could be used to scale the ever-present walls, and chains to rip off gates. We discussed vehicle-down drills, rehearsed with tow straps, and established "bump plans." We layered the bottom of the crew compartment with explosive-absorbing material, then we worked on building SOPs for traveling down the highway at night.

At this time in Iraq, the largest threat was remotely activated, wire-initiated IEDs, although they were nowhere near the threat they would become in later years. With the countermeasures we had in place to defeat RC devices, the main concern became pressure plates and wire-initiated IEDs.

There was little we could do about pressure plates, other than avoiding running over anything suspicious and altering routes as much as possible. To avoid man-activated bombs, we traveled at night, blacked out, using infrared headlights visible only to our goggles. And we drove fast.

Before deployment, Jon Laplume came through with AN/PVS-15 night-vision binoculars. These featured two tubes instead of the monocular night vision most non-SOF units were using. Binocular (two-eyed) vision gives you depth perception and an increased the field of view, which made them a vast improvement for driving—especially fast.

We drove in a staggered column when possible: one vehicle on each side of the road, with tight dispersion, and we moved as fast as the Humvees would go. Through our planning we had envisioned all the things we would need to do to be successful, as well as all the things that could go wrong. In our rehearsals we had choreographed the actions and reactions to each event and practiced them until we got them right, then continued to practice until we couldn't get it wrong. In my mind, attention to detail and the willingness to rehearse repeatedly is the hallmark of any professional organization.

At two o'clock in the morning there weren't many people on the road, and those who were likely to be there weren't up to any good. Eric drove the lead vehicle and I was second, with Ben manning the navigation computer in the passenger seat and working the radio to pass along information:

"Right turn in twenty-five hundred meters...
"Right turn in one thousand meters...
"Right turn in five hundred meters...
"Next right."

On a few occasions, we heard explosions behind us. A sleepy sentry had awakened to our engine noise but mashed the detonator too late.

***

Finally, on May 2, I was called in to the JOC. There was a mission. One of the intel guys had been poring over reports and had connected a seemingly unconnected series of events. Iraqi interpreters had been getting killed. As he began going back through the reports, he discovered that at separate locations around Baghdad, over a relatively short period of time, seventeen interpreters had been murdered. These were Iraqi citizens who volunteered to work with us. Working with coalition forces was dangerous profession, but seventeen was a lot, even in 2004 Baghdad. Due to our growing web of connections, the analysts were able to link this data with information from an FBI cell working out of the Green Zone. There was one employee who was connected to all seventeen of the dead. A woman.

The naming convention for missions used the first letter of the TU name to help the CJSOTF track operations. We were TU Raider, and the target was a woman, so our first mission was dubbed Operation Rachel, and we quickly began referring to the target by that name.

There was of course the expected food fight for the mission, but this was where my policy of "doing windows" paid off. Unfortunately, I couldn't take my team along. This was going to require a small footprint and certain unique skills. The mission had to be conducted in daylight, during working hours. We would be in civilian clothes and driving civilian vehicles. I was limited to two small sedans. I brought along a SEAL who knew the area; Scotty, one of our HUMINT folks; and Jack, the TL from Team Six. There also were the problems that searching a woman posed, so we reached out to the GROM and asked to borrow Kate.

In truth, it was expected to be a simple mission: drive to a building just outside of the Green Zone that housed the company "Rachel" worked for and where we expected to find her, walk in, confirm her identity, grab her, and get out.

We weren't necessarily concerned about the threat she posed, only that she might be being watched or have some level of security around her.

I briefed the team, and after a quick walkthrough we loaded the vehicles and set out. We arrived at the location, pulled into the parking lot, and while the others positioned themselves to maintain security, I walked inside with Kate. We asked for Rachel at the desk inside. The man at the desk recognized the name but told us that she was no longer working at that location. He dug through his files and told us that she had been sent to an army base some time ago to translate. He provided us with the unit's name.

I called back to the JOC on the sat phone, and they were able to come up with the unit's address—just a thirty-minute drive from our current location. Major Kozeniesky authorized me to continue. This scene played out over the morning. We arrived at a location, only to be told that she had moved just a week or two ago. At each location, they relayed that they missed her, and what a wonderful lady she was.

It was early afternoon when we finally arrived at the unit where she had most recently worked, translating for an army lawyer and his staff. The lawyer told us she had quit just days before. Finally, I confided in the major and explained why we were after her. He expressed disbelief that Rachel could be responsible for the deaths, but he agreed to our subterfuge and called her to come in to pick up her final paycheck.

She agreed and said that she would be right in. The Middle Eastern sense of time doesn't always work the same way that the Western world does. "Right in" might mean thirty minutes or four hours, but we established a plan and got ready. We anticipated that she would arrive with a driver, as it was unusual for women to drive. I sent Jack to the base gate to give us early warning, then positioned two us outside of the building. We were responsible for detaining the driver. Rachel would be allowed to enter the building and would be directed to an office where Kate was waiting to subdue and search her.

It was a little over an hour later that Jack's voice came through my headset. They had just come through the gate. Jack made sure that guards allowed them through. I notified the building's personnel to remain in their offices. After a short wait, the blue sedan pulled up to the front of the building. The woman who stepped out of the car was not what I was expecting. In her late forties, Rachel was poised and matronly. Gray tinged her black hair. As she entered the front of the building, the lawyer, eager to play a role in our caper, met her and directed her to the first-floor office. I didn't see what happened inside, but she was quickly subdued and searched by Kate while Scotty questioned her for time-sensitive information. Were there any assassinations imminent? Were there weapons or explosives in the vehicle? Was there anyone waiting outside the base to follow them? Rachel looked clueless in response to the questioning.

Meanwhile, outside, we detained the driver, pulling him from the car and searching him, then securing his hands with plastic flex-cuffs and pulling a hood over his head, then searching his car.

Moments later, Kate and Scotty led Rachel out of the building, cuffed and hooded, and placed her in the back of one of the other vehicles, separated from her driver.

I thanked the lawyer for his assistance and called the JOC to let them know we were on our way back to base.

We dropped off Rachel and the driver at a detention facility near the airport. We had the authority to hold detainees for a limited amount of time for questioning before we were required to transport them to the main detention facility at Abu Ghraib prison.

While it wasn't the most glamorous or dangerous of missions, it was our first, it was successful, and we hoped it would provide information that would allow us to find a chink in the armor of the terrorist cells that operated in and around Baghdad.

To the interrogators, it quickly became apparent that Rachel was not a criminal mastermind, but that did not mean that she had not been culpable in the translator deaths. It seemed that she had been duped into passing along lists of names and addresses of other translators to a "friend." With the shock of her capture and questioning, it took a while for the horror of what had happened and her role in it to sink in. Once it did, she was inconsolable, but provided information on "the friend" and was released.

Her driver knew the man we were now interested in and was willing to accompany us on the mission to identify him. So, we began planning Operation Racket.

The man in question lived with his wife and two children in a small, commercial/residential neighborhood on the outskirts of Baghdad. He owned a small appliance-repair shop just down the street from his house. And in his spare time, he built rockets that were being used against coalition forces, and he was at least tangentially involved in the interpreter murders.

We decided to hit the house and workshop simultaneously, with two assault teams attacking each objective. My team would be driving, and Jack's manning the vehicle's guns. Ben went to work planning routes. As I mentioned before, we tried to vary our comings and goings, but most routes had to include portions of "Route Irish," the nickname given to the 7.5-mile stretch from BIAP toward the Green Zone. During the much of coalition occupation of Iraq, it was also known as "the world's most dangerous road."

I went into planning with the other team leaders, studying maps to select the best spots to drop the assault force, which would proceed to the target on foot. At the designated spot, Eric in the lead vehicle and I behind him would turn left, while the remainder of the force continued down the street to the target house. We pulled over and allowed the assaulters to dismount and make their way around the corner to the shop. The glass of the store front was covered in a sliding metal gate secured with a massive padlock.

In my right ear I could hear the coordination taking place via radio as the breach team approached the home.

At the shop, the team was working through how to attack the giant lock. The hasp was too thick for the bolt cutters they carried.

At the house, the breacher was preparing to detonate his charge when one of the EOD techs saw a shadow cross in front of a window, headed for the front door. He ran forward, drove his arms through the window's glass, grabbed the shadow, and pulled it into the wall just as the breach exploded. This saved the shadow's life and made sure that we didn't inadvertently kill either the target or possibly an innocent.

The heavy crunch of the explosion was followed by two quick pops from "lock-busters," fired in rapid succession into the padlock from a sawed-off breaching shotgun. A lock-buster is a shotgun round that usually contains a frangible ceramic powder, or powdered steel in the place of pellets. They are designed to defeat a lock or hinges without the danger of over-penetrating and injuring someone in the room behind the door. The round ripped the lock from the door and the assaulters yanked the gate open. Then the breacher attacked the front door with a fireman's Halligan tool, a thick steel bar with several sets of prying teeth. Once the team made entry, Eric and I pulled our vehicles into the designated positions to provide security.

The raids were over in minutes. I followed along by the radio calls. The shop was small but full of material that had to be searched, while the house was larger and full of people. The man who had been grabbed at the breach point was pulled out into the street to the back of the armored vehicle where our source stood. The bag was pulled from his head and a bright light shined in his face, both to illuminate him and to prevent him from being able to identify the source. The source nodded, positively identifying the target. Once confirmation was received, his hood was replaced and he was loaded into a vehicle.

However, as we would rediscover often, identifications made under duress were sometimes incorrect. Back inside, the man's wife told us that the true target was hiding next door. The aircraft overhead confirmed that someone had slid over the wall just after the breach, and so the teams moved to clear the house next door. They found the target, the cousin of the man we had in custody, hiding there. The cousin we had in the truck, who bore a strong family resemblance, was released.

The streets were quiet at that time of night. The weather still sticky, but sometimes you could catch a breeze. In the warm months, entire families often slept on the roofs of houses on thin mattresses carried upstairs. After the explosion of the breach, I would see heads poke out over rooftops and small eyes wondering what had disturbed their sleep. Usually, they would quickly return to bed, or at least they would disappear, pulled away from the roof's edge by adults, and hurried inside until we had left.

Upon returning from a mission we got to work sorting through the material that had been taken from the objective, and transporting the detainees to the detention facility. On target, items that were suspected to be of intelligence value were bagged and marked according to the room or location they had been found: weapons, explosives, documents, computers, and often large sums of currency. Now, the intel analysts had to make sense of it all, ensuring the correct bags were assigned to the correct rooms and annotated on the floorplan sketch, and confirming which detainees had been found in which rooms, using a numbering system. Finally, they needed to confirm which assaulter had collected which items or grabbed which detainee.

Once they were satisfied that they had a handle on the information picture, we conducted a debrief. We reviewed the mission, from the start of planning through our return to base. Each key leader reviewed his decisions and actions, while everyone else looked for holes, information gaps, errors in thinking or action that could have resulted in mission failure.

It was necessary to have thick skin during debrief, but this was where we got better, by deliberately reviewing and critiquing each step of the mission, "Why did you think that?" "Why did you do that?" "What didn't you know that you should have?" "What should we have anticipated?" "What could we have done better?"

The debrief could go on for hours, but once complete, we turned to clean up. When we cleaned up after a mission, we followed the Marine mantras of "team before self" and "weapons, gear, body." We started with the crew-served weapons on the vehicles. They were pulled from their mounts, lugged into the common area, and cleaned and lubed before being returned to the large, metal shipping containers that served as our armory.

Then we turned to equipment—removing, cleaning, and storing the radios and electronics, and making sure they were ready to go for the next op. Vehicles were cleaned out, and if any equipment from the vehicle kit had been used, it was checked, cleaned, or replenished and replaced. Then we turned to individual weapons. Though they were seldom fired, except for the breaching shotguns, they were cleaned and operations-checked before being set aside.

Next, personal kit: refilling magazines, replenishing the bangs and the chemlights we used to mark clear rooms. Finally, when everything was ready for the next mission, we turned to showers, waiting around for a turn in the eight-shower trailer that served all of us. The water was tepid at best, but it was always too hot outside, and it was impossible for me to make it from the shower to my bedroom without picking up a thin sheen of sweat and a thick coat of Iraqi dust.

While we cleaned up, the intel analysts' work was just beginning. They dug through the information we brought from the objective—papers, computers, and thumb drives. Explosives were sent out to be tested to determine the country of origin. Computers that couldn't be accessed, or documents that had to be translated, were copied and sent to specialists. Meanwhile, the HUMINT guys were preparing themselves to talk with the detainee.

In most cases, the sun was rising by this point, with us third-shift workers clocking out and handing responsibility over to the first shift.

My key takeaway from the first weeks in-theater, and from the preparation and planning that went into Operations Rachel and Racket, was that it was the quality of the individual Marines and sailors that would make us successful: from the intel guys who dug through reams of information looking for connections, to the mechanics who kept our decrepit vehicles running, to the leadership that gave us left-and-right limits but room to run between them, to the individual assaulters on the teams, who recognized the criticality of the missions and would do whatever it took to make us successful.

I have since heard the analogy used of a basketball game in the final quarter as the clock ticks down the waning seconds, with the home team down by one. There are plenty of players who will hustle and run back and forth, never quite positioning themselves to take the throw-in. In the final five seconds, they don't really want the ball. They don't want the responsibility of performing under the enormity of the pressure, they don't want to be liable for the team's loss. That is human nature, and it can be understood. But there are a wonderful few who thrive in that chaos. Who beg for the ball, who want the shot.

This was what I had experienced in Afghanistan but had not been able to describe: when skill is slightly outmatched by requirement, and incredible performance is possible. It's called the flow state, and in it, with everything on the line, you become incredibly alive and entirely confident in your ability to execute.

We had a detachment full of guys who thrived in these situations.

CHAPTER 9
IT'S HARD TO BE GOOD

*I will never forget that I am an American, fighting
for freedom, responsible for my actions, and dedicated
to the principles which made my country free.*
—Article six of the US Armed
Forces Code of Conduct

I mentioned earlier that when we detained someone, we had a limited amount time to conduct interrogations. After roughly ninety-six hours we either had to let them go or take them to the Abu Ghraib Detention Facility. Abu G, as we called it, was less than a thirty-minute drive from Camp Myler. During the reign of Saddam Hussein, Abu G had been known as a site of torture and murder that many never returned from. The prison had been emptied and closed during the invasion, but reopened in August 2003 under coalition control.

When we were preparing to transport a detainee, we contacted the prison to let them know we were coming and who we were bringing, then we loaded up a convoy of sufficient size to provide security and set out. This was one of the times when we left the wire during daylight. When we arrived, we pulled our vehicles through the main entry gate and drove up a dirt road to the compound, stopping along a chain-link fence, the top laced in razor wire. A metal gate opened and one of the HUMINT Marines escorted the detainee inside. They crossed a narrow gravel courtyard, then entered a doorway in the side of the building.

We sat in the vehicles, or got out to stretch our legs, joked around, and waited. A few minutes later, the HUMINT Marine would walk out, load up, and we'd drive off.

At this point we had not yet heard the rumors about Abu G, but the allegations of abuse at the prison began in January 2004 when a soldier filed a report. In February, the army directed Major General Antonio Taguba to investigate, but the results of that investigation wouldn't be released until sometime in May.

It is likely that any inkling of what was going on within the prison walls was overshadowed by the events of March 31. At roughly 10:30 a.m., four American contractors working for Blackwater, a private military contract company, were traveling in two SUVs as security for a catering company going to pick up kitchen equipment from an Eighty-Second Airborne unit base in the town of Habbaniyah. Their route took them out of Baghdad on Route Eleven, past Abu Ghraib and through the town of Fallujah. As they entered the town, the route narrowed to a busy street filled with shops and markets, slowing them down. The ambush was initiated as they neared the edge of town.

I had worked briefly with one of the men, former SEAL Scott Helvenston, but didn't know him more than to say hello and make small talk. I do know that he and the others were well-trained professionals who were sent out on the mission without an adequate level of preparation or support. I've read that the insurgents believed the vehicles held CIA operatives, and that was the reason for the attack, although I can't know that for sure. I've also read that the insurgents believed that all contractors in Iraq (at the time nearly twenty thousand) were CIA operatives.

***

If you are driving and start getting shot at, the first rule is to keep moving. Don't stop. As long as the vehicle will move, you stay in it and keep going. There is security in speed. Earlier in my career, the Marine Corps sent me to a small racetrack in West Virginia not far from my hometown for counterterrorism driving training. One of the tests began with an instructor driving, allegedly to demonstrate a technique. I was distracted from the road by watching and listening to him as we rounded a blind corner to discover that we were the target of an ambush. The driver suddenly slumped over the wheel, unresponsive, with the vehicle traveling at a high rate of speed. As the front-seat passenger, I had to slide as far across the seat as possible to get hands on the wheel and feet on the pedals, pushing the deadweight of the driver back and out of the way, and deciding in an instant whether to drive through or around the ambush, or to slow to a safe speed to attempt a bootleg turn without flipping the car. I made sure that this training was part of our preparation for combat. We frequently practiced drills in which the front-seat passenger or gunner would take control of the vehicle from an incapacitated driver.

But these men were caught in a complex ambush, and either the vehicles were disabled, or for some other reason they stopped. A stationary vehicle is a bullet magnet. Some reports say that the follow vehicle was stopped first; it's likely that the lead vehicle was attempting to assist. This would be in keeping with the inviolable rule that supersedes all others: never leave a teammate behind.

Once the vehicles were stopped, the attackers—insurgents from a group calling themselves the Islamic Jihad Army—approached and fired into the passenger compartment, ensuring all occupants were dead. Truthfully, this was a blessing, because when the gunfire stopped, a mob began to form. Men and boys, worked into a frenzy of hatred, doused the SUVs with gasoline and set them ablaze.

As the flames grew, so too did the size of the mob. At some point they began pulling burning bodies from the vehicles. A *New York Times* article by Jeffery Gettleman, posted the day of the attack, describes a body being pulled apart by group of young men, while a taxi driver screamed, "Viva mujahedeen! Long live the resistance!" A boy of ten years stomped on a burned skull and cried out, "Where is Bush? Let him come and see this!"

The growing crowd began to chant, "Falluja is the graveyard of Americans!" The burned corpses were dragged to the town's iron bridge and the chants and shouts intensified as the bodies were hung from the bridge supports, the Euphrates River running beneath them.

Across the globe, photos and video of the attack played on television sets, preceded by warnings from TV newscasters of the graphic nature of the material.

The effect of this sort of attack on me and the Marines I knew was to strengthen our resolve to root out insurgent leaders, to seek retribution for Scott Helvenston, Jerry Zovko, Wesley Batalona, and Mike Teague. We were pissed and wanted payback. If Iraqis found peace, that was a fine byproduct, but (and I can only speak for myself) that was far from my primary concern. I wanted revenge.

The attack occurred less a week before the Marines of TU Raider began landing in Iraq. Needless to say, it left an impression and shaped our mindset upon our arrival.

***

In a seemingly unrelated event, on April 6, the day our first planeload landed, an American freelance radio-tower repairman, Nicholas Berg, was released from custody in Mosul, Iraq. He had been detained nearly two weeks earlier by either Iraqi and/or US forces for reasons that are not quite clear. When he was released, he was strongly encouraged to catch a flight back home. He did not. A few days after his release, around April 10, he was kidnapped by a group linked to al Qaeda.

I didn't know anything about Nicholas Berg at the time. There may have been mention of an American being taken, but I don't think I heard his name until early May. I was just arriving in country and getting sorted out. We had bigger fish to fry.

***

On April 28, in a *Sixty Minutes* interview, CBS News broke the story of the abuse at Abu Ghraib, showing the pictures that are now famous: a detainee hooded in black, standing in front of a yellow wall on an MRE box with wires attached to his fingertips; smiling female soldiers leading naked detainees around on leashes like dogs; and Dan Rather asking Brigadier General Mark Kimmitt, deputy director of coalition operations in Iraq, what had gone wrong.

"Frankly, I think all of us are disappointed by the actions of the few," said Kimmitt. "Every day, we love our soldiers, but frankly, some days we're not always proud of our soldiers."

"What can the Army say specifically to Iraqis and others who are going to see this and take it personally?" Rather asked.

"The first thing I'd say is we're appalled as well. These are our fellow soldiers. These are the people we work with every day, and they represent us. They wear the same uniform as us, and they let their fellow soldiers down... Our soldiers could be taken prisoner as well. And we expect our soldiers to be treated well by the adversary, by the enemy. And if we can't hold ourselves up as an example of how to treat people with dignity and respect...we can't ask that other nations do that to our soldiers as well. So, what would I tell the people of Iraq? This is wrong. This is reprehensible. But this is not representative of the 150,000 soldiers that are over here. I'd say the same thing to the American people...Don't judge your army based on the actions of a few."

While I suspect that most Americans were horrified by the photos, I do seem to recall an outpouring of support for the soldiers. There are always the cries that "We need to take the gloves off," or that "We can't win if we hold ourselves to a standard that the enemy doesn't keep"— that "The provisions of the Geneva Convention don't apply to terrorists," or, "We can't expect fair treatment from them, so why should we fight with one hand behind our back?"—and many other not wholly unjustified complaints and questions.

The possibility of stepping off the moral high road always exists in combat. In the heat and smoke of battle, when focused on surviving and keeping your buddies alive, it can be easy to take a wrong turn. That doesn't mean that ethical failings can be excused or ignored, but they can more easily be understood, and when adjudicating breaches of the law of war, all factors should certainly be considered.

But none of the above factors should have been in question at Abu Ghraib. It was like a Stanford Prison Experiment on a large scale, without even the pretense of supervision. Fresh-faced All-Americans from the Army Reserve's 372nd Military Police Company, when given a nudge, turned from soldiers into sadists, rapists, and tormentors.

Of course, military intelligence and the CIA have been blamed, and likely bear some culpability by endorsing and encouraging this behavior to "loosen up" the prisoners up for interrogation.

The US policy of "enhanced interrogation techniques" at that time has been debated ad nauseum, but even that doesn't and can't excuse the abject failure of leadership and the actions of each individual involved. Thinking back, I recall being disgusted by the activities at Abu G, but I believe my main concern was how those actions would impact our mission. It was an unforced error, a self-inflicted gunshot wound to the ideas and institutions we professed to fight for. If the Blackwater deaths strengthened my resolve to fight, why would the photos released from Abu Ghraib have any different effect on the enemy? And what is the effect on the civilian population when they come to believe that the cure the coalition was peddling seemed little better than the disease?

Now, to be fair, thousands were killed in Abu Ghraib under Saddam's rule, but moral justification can't be measured in degrees. Our adherence to *our* values must be the benchmark, not what the other guy is doing.

***

I honestly don't believe that I expended too much energy on the philosophical debate at the time. In our world, we were beginning to reap the benefits of Commander Wilson's decision to spread out our intelligence guys. We now had access to a far wider swath of information, and our guys were able to connect dots that no one else was seeing. The Task Force HQ served as the clearing house for information, and since we were in Baghdad, we had primacy of operations in that area. Additionally, we made connections with several of the Special Forces ODAs (Green Beret A-Teams) in the area, who were focused on intel collection but didn't have the manpower for executing full-scale raids. We offered to help and soon found ourselves working the night shift.

Most nights found us heading outside the wire conducting capture/kill missions on mid-to-high-value targets.

It was these intel connections that finally gave us a lead on the insurgent leader we knew only as "X." Through a paid source, they were able to begin tracking a van that was sometimes used to shuttle "X" around. He kept on the move, seldom sleeping in the same house twice, and scheduling meetings at far-flung locations around Baghdad where any military presence would be visible at a great distance.

***

On the morning of May 8, a coalition patrol pulled over to examine an orange bundle on an overpass outside of Baghdad. I'm sure that they were wary of IEDs, and that they stopped the vehicles some distance away, examined the immediate area for signs of wires or tampering, scanned the horizon for the glint of glass or hidden ambush positions. But eventually they moved forward to examine and identify the object. It was the headless body that would be identified as Nick Berg, dressed in an orange jumpsuit like those worn by Abu Ghraib prisoners.

Two days later, on May 11, anti-coalition forces released the video of Nick Berg's execution. A room with a yellow wall; five militants dressed in black, wearing headdresses and chest rigs holding AK magazines; Nick Berg in his orange jumpsuit. One of the men in black was suspected to be Abdullah Yasser Sabawi, a nephew of Saddam. The man who took a long knife and cut off Berg's head was allegedly Abu Musab al-Zarqawi, a name we knew well. His photo sat near the top of the insurgency hierarchy. Zarqawi was a Jordanian video-store clerk turned insurgent leader. By this time, he was one of the most wanted men on the planet. The video was posted online with the title, "Sheikh Abu Musab al-Zarqawi slaughters an American infidel with his own hands." I had no interest in watching the video, but the masked figures made it clear that the murder was in response to the atrocities at Abu Ghraib.

The same day the video was released, a source close to "X" passed us word that he was scheduled to attend a meeting at a house in downtown Baghdad. We named it Objective Red Bull. We sat sweating in our Humvees, waiting for the signal that he had arrived. The case officer in communication with the source sat staring at a burner cell phone, willing it to ring. When it finally did, the message was relayed and final confirmation received as a crackle over the radio—"You guys are green, GO!"—and we pulled out into the night.

The hit went flawlessly. We detained three men. The owner of the house was one of the secondary targets, a known bomb-maker. We loaded our vehicles with bomb-making components we pulled from the house. One of the other detainees was a bomber who had been wanted by coalition forces for some time. But somehow "X," if he had ever actually been there, had escaped again.

Days after the raid, one of our sources and his young daughter were executed in retaliation. This upped the urgency to find "X." We were casting a wide net for information and moving on all promising leads. Maybe we would find him; but if not, we could keep him off balance and work to shrink his base by making it costly for those who supported him.

Several days later, we got another possible location on "X." Objective Racoon consisted of three rural targets that had to be hit simultaneously. The missions went well, and we confiscated weapons, explosives, and documents. But once again, no "X." We did, however, detain several of his male family members, all of whom bore a strong familial resemblance. The intel folks felt that now, at least, we knew what he looked like, and again, the targets produced a treasure trove of bomb-making material.

Following the raid, a source close to "X," fearing reprisals, fled to Jordan, limiting our access to information.

A few days later, I was shaken awake and called early into the JOC. The SF ODA had uncovered some information on the Nick Berg murders. We went into planning for an early night raid on a third-floor apartment on the outskirts of Baghdad, which we dubbed Objective Revenge. We found one man asleep in the apartment, surrounded by evidence of the murder, and brought him in.

It was unusual for one of us assaulters to sit in on interrogations. Frankly, we had no place there, but I was curious. I wanted to try to understand what possessed these people—to know the level of belief or hate or commitment that it took to take part in atrocities like the Berg murder. I was also curious because the Abu G debacle had shown that our people were not immune from crossing clearly marked ethical boundaries. I volunteered to provide security during the interrogation.

There are so many levels of killing. The indiscriminate and anonymous bomb, whether it falls from an aircraft or is detonated from under the sand, is impersonal. Killing with a rifle, even at relatively close quarters, offers some psychic distance. But to murder someone who is restrained, who presents absolutely no threat, is a different thing entirely. Killing amid battle is fueled by a chemical cocktail of adrenaline, cortisol, and dopamine that floods the system. It had been my experience that killing was usually autonomic—acting without conscious thought, a response to a deadly stimulus. Unprovoked murder, on the other hand, must be fueled by either extreme hate, fear, or psychopathy.

I didn't want to think myself capable of that. To delight in the degradation of a live human is worse, in my opinion, than desecrating a corpse. I have always believed in a code of behavior, as silly as it may sound for someone whose life's work has been to actively seek out and kill those who are on another side of something. But at least they had the opportunity to participate.

***

By this time, we had our own temporary detention facility established. A large block building inside a walled area, just a short drive from our compound. The interrogation rooms were freshly painted white; the smell of paint still lingered. A square metal table bolted to the floor dominated a space that looked not unlike the interrogation room from an episode of *Law & Order*, minus the two-way mirror. My job was to stand in the corner, arms crossed and looking stern, as the detainee was escorted into the room. He wore a blue jump suit too long for him; its wrists and ankles were turned up. He also was cuffed at the wrists and ankles, shuffling forward, prodded by a guard. When he reached the table, his goggles were removed. He blinked against the bright fluorescent lights that hung in four rows from the ceiling above him. The guard pointed him to the waiting chair.

When the guard left and the door closed, he turned his head right, then left, trying to place himself, to see where he was and who was with him. When he saw me, he quickly turned his head to face the front. I didn't get a good look at him, but it was enough to remind me that demons seldom look like demons under the light. I wondered what I looked like to *him*. There was no reflective surface for me to get a look at myself, but suddenly I wished there were.

I moved slightly to take a position behind him so that he couldn't see me, for no other reason than to instill fear. After a wait that was longer than it seemed, Scotty opened the door and held it as the interpreter entered, then shut it behind them. The interpreter ("terp") walked to the table and took a seat to the left of the detainee. Scotty sat a bottle of water down, then took the seat to the detainee's right and placed a medium-sized cardboard box on the floor beside him.

Even when speaking through an interpreter, it is important to make eye contact with the person you're talking to. This is even more true when the person is being interrogated. Eyes speak volumes. Scotty turned to face him, leaning forward, his face inches from the detainee; as he moved, his chair legs screeched against the concrete floor. Everyone except Scotty flinched at the sound. He jumped right in.

"So, tell him we know he was involved in Nick Berg's murder."

The interpreter relayed the message. You didn't need to speak Arabic to understand the detainee was protesting the accusation, proclaiming his innocence.

"Who else was involved? He's going to have to give me names."

After the exchange, the terp turned to Scotty. "He says he is innocent. He knows nothing of what you are talking about."

Scotty nodded, then leaned over and pulled a stack of freshly burned DVDs from the box and slammed them on the table. "Ask him if he knows what these are. Ask him if he knows where they came from."

"He says he's never seen them before."

"Never seen them. That's funny, because we pulled them out of his apartment. Does he know what's on them?"

From my vantage point I couldn't see the fear that I knew crossed his face, but I could see the muscles in the back of his neck and shoulders tense like ropes. His leg shook against the table leg. I could see the fury in Scotty's eye that was only partially theater.

Scotty leaned to the box and pulled out a large Ziploc bag. He turned and slammed it down on the table, his fist crashing down and the thunder reverberating from the metal surface and rebounding off the walls. "How about this?" The pitch of his voice dropped to a booming whisper. "Ask him if he's seen this before."

The bag contained clothing and towels now brown with dried blood.

Without waiting for a reply, he turned once more and produced a laptop, opened it, and sat it on the table in front of the man. The video was cued and paused; lines of static ran across the screen; but there was no mistaking the scene depicted. Five men in black standing against a yellow wall, one man in orange kneeling in front.

I was pulled forward by a force I couldn't fight, repelled, but unable to return to my position at the wall. Unable to look away. I moved behind the detainee. I wrapped my hands around the metal chairback and gripped it as hard as I could.

He felt me there or perhaps sensed my presence. He tensed. I knew that he wondered if I was to be his executioner. I wanted him to believe that I was.

Before Scotty could push Play, the detainee began forcefully proclaiming his innocence, denying involvement, expressing through his body language horror at what was on the tape. I don't think it was an act. Even though we truly believe that he was involved in the murder, I think it is a far different thing to look back at the evidence. At the time, he had been caught up in the moment; now he sat cuffed in a room not so different from the one that came to life as Scotty pushed Play.

I didn't want to watch. I turned my head but couldn't keep the images from my peripheral vision. Then I gave in, turned, and watched. The force and violence and hate. The hacking. I thought I would be sick. I didn't make it to the end without closing my eyes. But with my eyes closed I could see myself slide my arm around his neck and tighten.

There are two types of chokes. The blood choke obstructs the carotid arteries on either side of the neck, reducing blood flow to the brain. The effect is like a television being turned off; the scene fades to black. It's not terribly unpleasant, and the subject recovers quickly once blood flow is restored. The other is the air choke. The target is the cricoid cartilage and the windpipe. It prevents the subject from taking in oxygen. It is painful, it induces terror, and it takes a long time.

That's what I wanted to do. I wanted to do it so badly. On the movie screen inside my head, my arm slid around his neck, turned so that the large radius bone ran across the front of his windpipe. I clasped my hands together and pulled, pressing my chest against his back for leverage. Delighted with the feel of cartilage collapsing. Feeling through my whole body as he gasped, shook, and struggled. His arms and legs slapping uselessly against the chair and the floor. I could see and feel the muscles in my shoulders begin to ache, but ignored them as my arms grew weary, until my shoulder muscles burned until I felt the cartilage give way under my forearm. I wanted to feel the spasms as his life seep away into final, weak flaps and kicks....

But I didn't do any of this. I just gripped the back rail of his chair so hard I thought I would leave marks in the metal.

The concept of *jus in bello*, or "right conduct in war," has been likened to handing out speeding tickets at a NASCAR race. But it is necessary. The moment that an enemy combatant surrenders or can no longer fight, we have a duty to try to protect them from harm and provide medical treatment. We do not have the obligation to hazard our personnel to do so, or to provide treatment to him before one of our own, but our obligations are clearly enshrined in law.

We have lists of rules, ranging from the esoteric Just War theory of Thomas Aquinas, to international humanitarian law. These are parsed and fretted over by lawyers to pen Rules of Engagement, based on the environment, the mission, and its criticality. If we pick and choose when we follow these rules, it isn't a matter of not being better than those we are fighting; it is a matter of not living up to the ideas we swore to protect, the values we profess to be supporting and defending. And if those ideas aren't what we are defending, what is it all for?

Marcus Aurelius said, "The best revenge is not to be like your enemy." But I think if I had been granted permission at that moment, I would have killed him there, cuffed, helpless. I wanted so badly to have him die by my hand. But that desire, and the hate that formed it, burned up fast and hot, and I was left with a sick feeling in my stomach. Sick certainly for Nick Berg, but for myself as well. What is more, at that moment I knew I was capable of evil. And I have come to suspect that given the right set of cues and circumstances, we are all capable of it.

CHAPTER 10

GOOD AT WAR

*Today is only one day in all the days that will
ever be. But what will happen in all the other
days that ever come can depend on what you do
today. It's been that way all this year. It's been
that way so many times. All of war is that way.*
—Ernest Hemingway, *For Whom the Bell Tolls*

As the neighborhood slept, our line of vehicles crept through the narrow residential side streets on the outskirts of Baghdad. We drove blacked-out, relying on infrared headlights and night-vision goggles to negotiate the tight turns. In the turrets, gunners alternated fields of fire. The muzzles of .50 caliber machine guns and 40-millimeter grenade launchers pointed into the darkness, slowly swaying back and forth like charmed cobras, an instant from spitting death. Each man in the open-backed vehicles scanned rooftops and blind corners, M4 carbine barrels protruding like porcupine quills. As we raced down the highway leading to this place, the helicopters that provided overwatch held back, turning slow circles in the sky, far enough away to prevent disturbing the early morning quiet.

I was driving the second vehicle. We were responsible for navigation. Ben sat in the passenger seat, his head buried in a laptop screen. "Next right, and the second left." His whisper crackled through fifty radio headsets.

Each team named their gun truck using the theme of war gods. We stenciled the names in big block letters with flat-black paint along the front fenders to distinguish them: Thor, Odin, Mars, Ares, Juno, and Tyr. We picked old gods of legend and lore. No one suggested just "God" or "Allah." While I'm sure that proposal wouldn't have been appreciated, there is certainly the case to be made that they are the biggest war gods of all. We have fought in their names for millennia, and this desert sand has swallowed more than its share of blood.

In the lead vehicle, Eric slowed and made the turn, expertly threading the seven-foot-wide, nearly four-ton armored vehicle between parked cars. I followed, and behind me the remainder of the assault force. Just before the final turn, he pressed the brakes and came to a stop, the breach team already scrambling from the back.

The ends of our metal ladders were covered in scraps of carpet and wrapped in the olive-drab military version of duct tape. Carried on hooks on the side of our vehicles like fire trucks. Ready to be lifted off and used to scale a wall, if required. There was always a wall. Once in a great while it was waist-high and could be vaulted; but usually they were tall—eight feet or more. The tops covered in broken glass bottles.

We tried to know if there was a wall, where the gate was, and the layout of the house, if we could. Sometimes it was possible to get overhead coverage from an Unmanned Aerial Vehicle (UAV), or to have someone, preferably a trusted Iraqi, drive by in a vehicle set up with hidden video cameras. But the targets we hunted were skittish. It was because of their wariness that they were still alive and still free. They seldom stayed in the same house for more than a day or two, and they often employed locals to keep an eye out for anything suspicious. They would flee at the first indication that something was amiss.

This target was warier than most, so we didn't attempt a drive-by. He had been an intelligence officer under Saddam. Now he was a leader in what we called the FRE—former regime elements fighting to prevent the upcoming transfer of sovereignty from coalition control into the hands of the Iraqi interim government. The mission had been dubbed Objective Ricochet.

The typical city block in the communities around Baghdad was two lots wide and often ten or more lots long. Homes were generally set to the back of the lot, to create a small front yard sometimes used for a garden. The flat-roofed buildings typically filled the full width of the lot, so that when seen from above, the block appeared to be one massive, multi-angular building. Quite often the block was full of an extended family unit willing to go to any lengths to hide a nephew, cousin, or uncle from us. It only took seconds for a tipped-off target to clamber from rooftop to rooftop and disappear in the labyrinth of semi-connected structures.

Sid's team placed the ladders against the wall. The first man climbed just until he could poke his muzzle over the top to pull security, sweeping the front of the house until someone negotiated another ladder and dropped into the yard below. Then they flowed over the wall, one after another, until there were enough to secure the front of the building and place the breaching charge. Terry's team was in the lead. Once they were over, they pressed forward, weapons covering danger areas, moving in a crouch toward the building, lifting their feet high to avoid stumbling over a child's toy or garden tool.

Chess is often touted as a metaphor for war. It is based on the elephants, chariots, and infantrymen of sixth-century India. It's a "perfect information game." This means that each player has access to all available information, the only difference lying in the knowledge of strategy. For those crafting strategy, there may be some value in learning chess, but I've never been fond of it. Combat is far from a "perfect information game." For the man with sand in his boots and a rifle in his hands, combat more closely resembles checkers. You move forward and avoid getting jumped. The goal is to make your opponent play blindfolded, sleepy, and force him to move so quickly that he makes mistakes.

The secret to being good at war is really just geometry. You need to understand the angles you can be shot at from, then position yourself to minimize those angles, preferably behind something hard. Then you prioritize those angles you can't minimize by estimating the likelihood of a bad guy being there, and you point your rifle at the most likely threat.

When you have a group of men on your side all doing the same thing, it's efficient, deadly, and beautiful to watch. Choreographed chaos.

Early in my career, I had a team leader who told me about a high-school summer that he spent working with a touring carnival as a roust-about. When he had difficulty completing a job he had been assigned, the carnie in charge would show him and tell him each time, "It's all about techniques and angles." We were drinking when he told me that story, but it stuck with me. I have since come to view the old carnie's words as a mantra. If your technique doesn't work, come at the problem from a new angle. And each time the new angle works, you've added a technique to your toolbox.

From my driver's seat, I waited for the radio call, "Breaching, breaching, breaching!" That was immediately followed by the thump of an explosive charge on the door, which was the signal for our vehicles to roar forward. In Thor and Ares, the drivers floored their vehicles to reach the northwest corner of the block, while Mars and Tyr locked down the southeast corner. From these opposing corners, with two vehicles and mounted machine guns, they could effectively isolate and contain the objective area—meaning that they would be able to see and react to anyone trying to flee, or anyone sneaking in to jump us.

The helicopters, which had been holding off to retain our surprise, were nose forward, pushing to the objective to provide an over-head view and report any activity, using a homemade map we called a GRG—a gridded reference graphic. The GRG was an overhead, pho-to-turned checkerboard with color codes and numbered and lettered reference lines, which made passing information quick and easy.

I pulled up on the street in front of the objective. I was followed by the command-and-control vehicles containing our boss, Major Kozeniesky; the Joint Terminal Air Controllers (JTACs), who were responsible for directing the helicopters; and the Explosive Ordinance Disposal (EOD) and intel folks, who would go on-target once it was secured. Smoke from the explosives hung in the air like a stratus cloud, and the smell of a million matchheads lingered. This was a process we had rehearsed and executed dozens of times in training and on missions.

Everyone knew what they were doing, and everything went like clock-work...until it didn't.

Things actually went very wrong as soon as Andy initiated the charge, but for those of us outside the compound, it took a few seconds to catch up. Andy made his way up to the door, looking for the material (wood or metal), the construction, the hinge side, the locking mechanisms, and many other factors that needed to be identified in a split second to allow for proper charge selection and placement.

When an explosive charge detonates, it creates an overpressure shockwave. The overpressure can rupture eardrums, lungs, and other soft organs if you are too close. The door sat under a covered awning, so Andy also had to consider reflective overpressure: the shockwave can bounce off walls and ceilings and redirect back toward the team. Finally, he needed to look for potential projectiles, anything near the breach site that might be hurled into the stack. Taking all of this into consideration, Andy positioned the team in a safe location eight feet away from the door. While he focused on the problem, another Marine provided security, prepared in case the door suddenly opened.

This night the door was made of heavy wood. Andy placed his charge to attack the lock side, then played out the thin "shock tube" detonation cord as he backed off to a safe spot around the corner. When he was set, the others peeled off their security positions and fell in line. Once the last man reached safety, Andy made the "breaching" call, the bright flash momentarily lit the night, and the low thump reverberated down the block.

And Andy fell to the ground, wounded.

There was a saying beaten into our brains by Colonel Coates: "In combat, you will not rise to the occasion, you will default to your level of training."

Once the adrenaline surges, experiential thinking takes over. You do what you have done in similar situations. If you have trained hard and well, then that is how you will perform. Inside the compound, that is what they did. Terry rushed forward to the door, and seeing it still there, he called first for tools: the sledgehammer, and a fireman's prying tool named for its inventor, Hugh Halligan. Over time the name had been perverted to the "Hooligan tool," due to the mischief it was capable of performing. When they discovered that the tools wouldn't be able to make quick work of the door, Terry called for the alternate breacher who placed his charge and detonated it, sending the thick door splintering into the home. As the team flooded into the building, the final man—the team corpsman, Tim—quickly assessed Andy, dropped a tourniquet on his chest, said, "Get that on your arm," then followed his team into the building.

We had rehearsed this scenario repeatedly. At the breach, the focus of effort must be establishing a foothold in the building. If someone goes down, they had to be stepped over or around. It wasn't that the team didn't care for Andy, but each second wasted gave the target time to plan his next move and find a way to get the jump on us.

The team flowed into the house, an irresistible force. Pairs splitting off, clearing rooms as they went. Terry paused at a closed door as rounds began pouring through it into the main room. Another corpsman, Mike, was hit in the lower leg but continued to clear the building, allowing himself to receive medical attention only after the house was clear. Glen fell in behind Terry and flung a flashbang into the room. They followed the blast into the room. Against the back wall, ascending a stairway, the target turned back and raised his weapon. Glen engaged and "Ricochet" tumbled down the steps, his blood painting the wall behind him, and fell lifeless on the tile floor.

Outside, my team corpsman, Doc Arnold, was working on Andy, who was still conscious and asking about the status of his reproductive organs (which were thankfully unharmed). Andy's communications headset had been removed along with his gear, as Doc worked to stabilize him for transport, so he was not privy to the ongoing radio communications telling us that Ricochet had been killed; but he did hear the gunfire pulsing from inside, and then the verbal call for a body bag as the morphine was being administered; and though he couldn't form the words to ask, he was medevaced unsure if the bag was for one of his teammates.

I have mentioned that gunfights create a time distortion. Most of the times I have been shot at, my perception of time has immediately slowed down. I feel that I am moving, thinking, and acting at my normal pace, but everything around me has ground to a crawl. I am certainly not alone in this; it is a common experience. The limbic system takes over the tasks that have been perfected and handed off to the subconscious, leaving the prefrontal cortex unencumbered to process more important information, or sometimes, to spin its wheels with random thoughts unsuited for a gunfight.

We loaded Andy's stretcher into my vehicle, and Hays, our signals intelligence leader, led the way in his gun truck, headed for the prearranged landing zone—an empty lot a few blocks away that we had selected from satellite imagery. I followed, while in the back Arnold worked to stabilize Andy.

The helicopter made it there before we did and sent out a call to let us know that the planned LZ was fouled with wires running across it and with several desert-colored concrete blocks not visible in the photographs. They lifted back up and headed out in search of a suitable landing area nearby. We followed them as best as possible until they called, letting us know that they had found a site a few blocks away.

Doc Arnold was reassessing Andy, looking for any bleeding that hadn't been controlled, checking his pupils, speaking to him in a reassuring voice. "Hey Andy, do you know where you are? You're looking good, buddy." He monitored his blood pressure and mental status.

As we pulled into the lot, the Blackhawk was dropping straight down into a clearing barely large enough to admit their rotors. The gunners leaned out over the skids, tethered to the aircraft by a rugged gunner's belt. The green glow of their night vision illuminated their stern faces. They passed information about the blind spots to the pilot. "Twenty-five feet...twenty-five feet...come left ten...OK, straight down...ten feet...five feet...we're down." The helo slammed to the ground and enveloped us all in a cloud of dust.

We unloaded Andy and ran with his stretcher to the open door of the helo, the rotors chopping the night air and kicking up fine sand. It was like walking into a heated cheese grater. The crew chief helped us get Andy aboard, and Doc jumped in with him. I squeezed Andy's boot, not knowing what else to do, and muttered to him that he would be fine, but the rotors ripped my words away.

We ran back to the truck as the pitch of the roar surged and the bird fought against gravity to lift up, and out of the zone. It headed for the Thirty-First Combat Support Hospital in Baghdad, whose doctors, nurses, and medics at the time were treating nearly one thousand casualties per month.

We returned to the target building. Things were wrapping up. The house was methodically searched, evidence was bagged and documented. Boxes of files, hard drives, bags of cash, and cell phones were being collected to hand over to the intelligence team. We left the house generally as we found it, save for the shattered front door and the pool of blood threading its way through the grout lines.

I told them to put the body bag in my vehicle. It was already stained with Andy's blood; no sense dirtying up another GMV.

Normally, when we returned from a mission, we would take any detainees to a holding facility for interrogation, and then conduct a debrief with the intel analysts and sort through the stuff we had taken from the objective, to review the documentation, answer their questions, and ensure that everything was accurate. If we had taken weapons or samples of explosives, they were tested and secured appropriately. But I needed to hose out the back of the truck; it had Andy's blood all over it. That was not something I needed everyone looking at and thinking about in the light of day. First, though, we needed to do something with the dead guy. Scotty arrived to take him off of my hands but needed help with the PID—Positive Identification.

A body bag looks like a sleeping bag made of thick, black rubber, with a shiny brass zipper running its length and carrying handles stitched into the sides. There are the usual government instructions, the part number, and other information stenciled neatly on the side in white—ALL CAPS. I had latex gloves on, and the bag was slick and sticky with blood. Fortunately, they provide a loop of material on the zipper. I had to stick my ring finger through to get a grip. Since I already needed a shower, I took swabs for DNA and inked and printed the dead guy's fingers.

"Thanks," Scotty said, "but I can't get a good photo like this."

The standard assault rifle for special operations is the M4 carbine. It fires a .223 caliber projectile. This is really very small, but it travels at 2,900 feet per second. The human head is an enclosed space, filled with cerebrospinal fluid meant to serve as a shock absorber for the brain; but fluid can't compress. This means that the bullet's impact can sometimes cause the skull to fragment. So, I had to do my best to rummage through the bag to find the elusive chunks of skull.

It was times like these, when we battled revulsion, that the darkest humor emerged. While I struggled to piece Ricochet together again for his photo op, Jon Laplume wandered out to see if he could lend a hand. I just shook my head and bastardized a line by Jules (played by Samuel Jackson) from the film *Pulp Fiction*: "Jonny, every time my fingers touch brain, I'm Superfly TNT! In fact, what the fuck am I doing on brain detail?" He laughed and got the hose. What else can you do?

I could write a book about the absolutely twisted and inappropriate humor prevalent in the military. But suffice it to say that one lesson I have learned is that in difficult situations, calm breeds calm just as surely as panic breeds panic. In the same vein, humor—the darker and more wildly warped, the better—is a grounding rod that reduces the horror, the self-pity, and pulls people out of their own heads, which in those times can be a place you do not want to be. If you can laugh, you can do what needs to be done. You can carry on. You can fight.

Thinking back about Ricochet now, it is impossible to muster an ounce of sympathy. I can't even remember his name, though I'm sure we were told it. I have no idea where his body was taken, but I know it would have been held for the family to claim and bury. This was far better treatment than was received by the fifteen thousand Feyli Kurds whose remains have never been found, or the 148 Shiite men and boys in the village of Dujail, or the countless others heaped into mass graves by Saddam's Ba'athist government, of which Ricochet was a part. So, while Saddam sat in a cell in Baghdad, Ricochet and others like him still fought to deprive their countrymen and women of the opportunity for an elected government. Any operation that allowed us to remove one of the FRE from the playing field was a success, even though this one came at a cost.

Normally, after work was done, I'd grab some breakfast and then gather in someone's room to have an illegal beer and watch a bootleg copy of season five of *The Sopranos*. That morning I skipped breakfast, took a long shower, and joined the others waiting up for word on Andy.

After he had been stabilized at the Thirty-First CSH, he was put on a C-5 to Landstuhl, Germany, and eventually made his way back to the States to recover.

Later we pieced together the events of the night. As Andy placed the charge, the Marine providing security turned away to investigate a noise at the corner of the house. So, he didn't see a portion of the charge pull free from the door as Andy turned away. The explosives, which were backed with adhesive tape, stuck to Andy's vest under his arm. When Andy initiated the charge, a portion of it exploded against his body. While his ballistic vest saved his life, he sustained serious injuries to his side, right arm, and leg.

By the time the rest of us returned home in October, he was back to training for triathlons. Andy would later serve as a plank-owner in the First Marine Raider Battalion.

Two days later, on May 28, we were told to stand down from hunting insurgents and to prepare for what the Naval Special Warfare Task Group commander, Commander Bill Wilson, called, "The most important mission in Iraq."

CHAPTER 11

THE MOST IMPORTANT MISSION

Be soft and calm but strong enough to break a spear
Like Abdullah's pen,
A grenade's thunder in Hassan's jugular poems.
Speak up at the assembly, like a man.
Be a shepherd like Moses.
Don't bow before Pharaoh on the throne of the deal
Like his right-hand man.
Stand proud.
—Kurdish poet Khider Kosari

When we learned that we would be going to Iraq, I started reading. To be honest, all I knew was what little I learned during the TV coverage of the Gulf War. As I mentioned, I missed the whole thing because I was assigned to embassy duty. All in all, it was a pretty good tradeoff. I spent two and a half years living abroad in Budapest, Hungary and Buenos Aires, Argentina. I had a great time and met Tracy, but I couldn't help feeling ashamed for missing out. This time I dug into the history.

***

The lines on the map that now define Iraq once held Mesopotamia, which in Greek meant "the land between the rivers," a portion of the Fertile Crescent that was fed by the Tigris and Euphrates Rivers. This was part of the land that helped make possible the Neolithic Revolution. Hunters and gathers gradually became farmers and animal domesticators, beginning around 10,000 BCE.

The land has gone by many names—Sumer, Babylon, Assyria—and has been ruled by many leaders and kings: from the mighty Hammurabi, who established the first written law and enshrined the idea of a presumption of innocence, to Cyrus the Great, Alexander of Macedon, the Roman emperor Trajan, and the Mongol ruler Hulagu Khan.

In the third century, the land was divided. Upper Mesopotamia, which included portions of current Syria and Turkey, took the name Al-Jazirah (the island), and lower Mesopotamia took the name Iraq-I Arab (escarpment of the Arabs).

The prophet Muhammad was born around 570 CE in Mecca and was raised by his grandfather and his paternal uncle, Abu Talib. When he was forty, Muhammad reported being visited by the angel Gabriel and receiving his first vision from God. Although it took a while, he developed a following, and by his death in 632 CE most of the Arabian Peninsula had converted to Islam.

It was after his death that the trouble that still plagues the region began. The succession of power over the Islamic religion was an ugly one. Some believed that Ali ibn Abi Talib, the son of Muhammad's uncle Abu Talib, should succeed Muhammad. Others supported Abu Bakir, one of the first converts to Islam, who was among Muhammad's closest companions.

Ultimately, Abu Bakr assumed leadership of the Muslim community as the first Rashidun caliph (the first four leaders to succeed Muhammad), and though his reign lasted for barely two years before his death, he would be the only Rashidun caliph to die of natural causes.

This line of followers believed in the righteousness of this succession and took the name Sunni, meaning "lawful" or "way."

Eventually, Ali ibn Abi Talib was named the fourth and final caliph of the Rashidun Caliphate. His followers would come to be known as shi'atu Ali, or partisans of Ali, now known as Shia. They believed that the bloodline of Muhammad should be followed in selecting new leaders.

Ali was assassinated in 661 in a plot meant to end the civil war that was dividing the factions of Islam. Eventually, an incredibly important mosque bearing his name would be built in the city of An Najaf. I'll talk more about An Najaf later.

The history of the area we now know as Iraq was tumultuous. By the sixteenth century, its inhabitants were caught in the middle of the conflict between the growing Ottoman Empire and the Safavid Empire in Iran. The Safavids declared that Shia would be the official religion of the empire and wanted to control Mesopotamia, because it was home to An Najaf and Karbala, both holy sites, and because Baghdad, which had once been the seat of the Abbasid Empire, held great significance. The Ottomans wanted to prevent Shia Islam from spreading into Asia Minor, and so they kept Mesopotamia as a buffer Sunni state.

The ongoing wars served to deepen the Shia-Sunni schism, and although the Shia population in Iraq was significantly greater, they were prohibited from holding positions of power. This led to the much smaller Sunni population gaining political and administrative experience, which allowed them to maintain control of the country into the twenty-first century.

Today there are an estimated 1.9 billion Muslims worldwide. Nearly ninety percent are Sunnis, and the other 10 percent are Shia. In Iraq, the percentages differ. Over 60 percent are Shia, but despite the percentages, the Sunnis managed to maintain power.

Following WWI, the Ottoman Empire was abolished, and the region's new borders were drawn in the Sykes-Picot Agreement. In 1920 the area became a League of Nations Mandate under the control of the British, and the name was changed from Mesopotamia to the "State of Iraq."

One of the significant impacts of these arbitrarily drawn borders was to eliminate the nation of Kurdistan, leaving its people split between Iran, Iraq, and Syria, with a large diaspora in Turkey. This has led to the Kurdish population being spread across these countries and at best shunned, or at worst actively attacked and murdered. Saddam was especially brutal in dealings with the Iraqi Kurdish population. In one 1988 attack, he was accused of using chemical munitions to kill and injure over fifteen thousand Kurds.

Following WWI, Britain imposed a Hashemite monarchy, meaning that it was led by descendants of Muhammad, and eventually Iraq gained its independence in 1932. After an April 1941 coup d'état by a military faction, the Iraqi government sided with the Nazis at the opening of WWII until the British reestablished control. Saddam Hussein, who was a child at the time, was apparently deeply impacted by this, as the uncle who raised him had his military career ended when the coup was crushed.

In 1945, during the final stages of World War II, Iraq joined the United Nations and became a founding member of the Arab League. Thirteen years later, in a 1958 revolution, military officers overthrew the Hashemite monarchy and established Iraq as a republic, which lasted all of five years before the Ba'athists seized control in 1963. Finally, in 1979, Saddam officially took power.

In 1995, after sixteen years in charge, Saddam held Iraq's first presidential referendum. Voters were issued ballots requiring them to list the names of their relatives. The connotation was clear. The next day, the people were notified that Saddam won the referendum with 99.96 percent of the votes. In the 2002 referendum, Saddam achieved a full 100 percent of the votes, and so his reign continued unchallenged until the 2003 coalition invasion forced him into hiding. On December 13, 2003, Saddam was pulled, disheveled, from a hole in his hometown of Tikrit.

***

Since the invasion, Iraq had been governed by the Coalition Provisional Authority (CPA), but now an Iraqi Interim Government (IIG) was to be appointed to prepare the way for free and open elections, which were set to take place in January 2005, after we had returned home. I later remembered watching from California on TV as Iraqi citizens displayed purple fingers, indicating that they had voted in the first free election anyone could remember.

The IIG was set to be established in late June 2004. It would consist of a president, two vice presidents, a prime minister, deputy prime minister for national security, and thirty cabinet ministers. This was the first step in making free elections possible. For the elections to be legitimate, they needed to be planned and overseen by Iraqis, not Americans. But before that could happen, we had to keep the members of the IIG alive at a time when a whole lot of people wanted them dead.

This is what Commander Wilson meant when he said we were taking on the most important mission in Iraq. We would be joining the other SEAL task units in providing personal security details (PSDs) for the leaders of the IIG.

We were not strangers to conducting PSDs. They were a mission most of us had been assigned in the past. In the days after 9/11, I ran a detail to protect the MEU commander and navy commodore during a quick visit to the country of East Timor. It wasn't a common mission or one we routinely trained for, but when a PSD was needed, we were usually the ones given it. In one way it made sense. We possessed some of the necessary traits: methodical planning, the ability to act calmly and resolutely under stress, and we could shoot really well. These are all skills needed to get our principal out of harm's way, or "off of the X," as we called it.

On the other hand, we were trained to be single-minded. When presented with a threat, we destroyed it, at all costs. This can be problematic when the mission is to keep someone alive. The job is not to kill the bad guy, or prevent him from hurting others, or even prevent him from hurting your teammates; it is to protect one person, the principal, above all else.

All other operations were put on hold and SEAL teams from across Iraq converged on Baghdad to prepare. We brushed up on the things we could expect, taught each other classes, and began rehearsing. A PSD consists of three components: drivers, the "body bunker," and an advance team. The drivers need to be the best you have. They will have to be able to keep their heads and drive through ambushes. The body-bunker guys will move with the principal whenever he is out of the vehicle. They are present for receiving lines, hang out in the background of lunches, and stand outside the door during meetings. I was tasked with leading the advance team. We were responsible for planning and checking routes, running coordination, developing contingency plans, and conducting security sweeps of sites before the principals were allowed in.

We never talked about whether we would die for our buddies. I don't think I gave it much thought, because I felt invincible. But sometimes I pictured a grenade sailing through a window or over the parapet of a roof and landing among my team, and I wondered if I would jump on it. I don't think that is the sort of thing you can plan for. I would picture myself grabbing the grenade and throwing it back, ducking as it exploded just out of harm's way. But in a PSD, it is your job to cover the principal, to put yourself between them and the bullets when the shooting starts. To form a body bunker and get them off the "X."

TU Raider was assigned to protect the Kurdish vice president of the IIG, Dr. Rowsch Shaways. Kurds were still viewed unfavorably by most Iraqis, so there were plenty of people who wanted him dead. I first met Dr. Shaways on the evening before the first meeting of the IIG. We had planned a route to pick him up from where he was staying in Baghdad and transport him to the Al-Rasheed (now the Royal Tulip) Hotel. We passed this route off to the team responsible for his security and moved to the hotel to prepare for his arrival.

The Personal Security Detail (PSD) for Vice President Shaways. (Several faces have been obscured for security.)

The Al Rasheed gained notoriety during the Gulf War when CNN used the site for its newscasts. Following the war, Saddam ordered a tile mosaic of George Bush to be placed on the lobby floor. This meant that visitors would walk over his face when entering, a sign of great disrespect. The mosaic was removed by soldiers after the invasion and replaced with a photo of Saddam. The lobby floor was covered by carpets on the day I arrived.

The Al Rasheed stood near the bank of the Tigris. It had taken several Scud missile hits in the early days of the war and was now largely unoccupied, but the undamaged sections were still in use by US personnel. Several months before we arrived, a rocket attack killed one service member and injured a dozen others.

We established a room for the vice president and his brother, who was traveling with him, then took rooms on either side and posted security at his door. My first meeting was brief. I could see in his eyes that he was tired. He shook our hands and thanked us for watching over him, then headed to bed. His brother spoke with us, and I listened to his security concerns and reviewed our procedures with him. When we were sitting and talking alone, I asked his brother if he was scared. "Me, yes. I'm scared for him because he won't be scared for himself."

The Shaways family had a tradition of service. Their father, Nuri Shaways, was one of the first Kurdish cabinet ministers in Iraq, and their mother, Nahida Sheikhsalam, was the first woman to serve as a member of Parliament. Dr. Shaways earned a doctorate in engineering in Germany and returned to Iraq in 1975 to join the Kurdish resistance to Saddam Hussein by leading Peshmerga forces in many battles. The Peshmerga have a fierce reputation as fighters. Their name means "those who face death."

Whenever I have been a part of a PSD, I have thought of a line from the Clint Eastwood movie *In the Line of Fire*. "All someone needs is a willingness to trade his life for the president's, right?"

It is probably true.

I have had the pleasure to watch the Secret Service work on several locations when I have been on the periphery of presidential visits. With their training, intelligence-gathering, authority, and resources, they operate at a different level, one we couldn't begin to match. So rather than worry about the myriad things I had no control over, I chose to take a cue from the Stoics and focus on the things in my power, and make sure we were doing our best to control them.

For us, the biggest threat were IEDs along the route or at a venue. To counter these, we planned multiple routes and only selected the final route at the last minute, so the secret was kept close-hold. I arrived at venues early with explosive ordinance disposal techs to sweep the building for any trace of explosives. That left attack from a distance by rocket, mortar, or sniper, so the intel guys plotted high points and lines of fire and we checked them. We limited exposure between the vehicle and venue and moved the principal in a body bunker, surrounded by shooters. Dr. Shaways was offered body armor which he usually refused to wear. He also wasn't fond of being surrounded by hulking Americans in body armor, which for us was both refreshing and maddening.

The next danger is the up-close threat of receiving lines and crowds. The first priority is to limit this, when possible, then control the crowd using barricades, when not. In a perfect world, we would be able to vet everyone in the crowd, but that is not realistic. Instead, we placed shooters on either side of the V.P., laser-focused on hands. Fortunately, we didn't have to deal with too many crowds.

Just as we were getting into the rhythm of managing the PSD, a new lead popped up on "X." We received information that he was planning a high-profile attack against the very men we were protecting. There also had been a recent spike in bombings, so we turned over responsibility for Dr. Shaways to the SEALs and returned to Camp Mylar. There we launched a concerted effort to target "X," as well as any other bomb-makers we could find, to try to keep the IIG alive until the planned transfer of sovereignty, scheduled for June 30.

The Task Group had managed to replace our aging Humvees with new GMVs. These were updated, special-operations variants with better armor, more power, greater range, and hardened components. And now I didn't have to worry about driving to the target. We handed off driving responsibility to another team and took our place in the assault. One of the things I noticed was that now I had a little more time to think. When I was driving, I had to be totally focused on the road, the vehicles around me, and the radio, but now I sat in a seat behind the driver with less to worry about.

If you let your mind run, it tends to wander to dark places. Almost everything can be controlled through good planning, preparation, and rehearsals. The one constant, lingering unknown is the IED. It's hard not to let the thought slip, and once you do it can become all-consuming. Every second waiting, expecting to disappear in a deep raw thump of fire and smoke, leaving others to stare into the crater that was a Humvee seconds before, or perhaps trying to cut and pull some or most of you from the twisted metal and burning cloth and fuel. Struggling with pressure dressings and tourniquets tightening above jagged amputations. Loud reassurances and whispers of concern. The fear, if left unchecked, can play in a loop on the mind's movie screen, resetting at each street intersection. The trick is to keep the thought from starting, which is like trying to avoid thinking of an elephant when someone tells you not to think of an elephant.

I tried to keep my mind focused on the route, mentally ticking off checkpoints as we passed them. In between checkpoints, I ran through a mental rehearsal. For me it was like observing from above—vehicles hitting their positions, assaulters disembarking and setting the breach. While I did this, I practiced deep breathing. I used a technique called "box-breathing" to calm myself and bring focus. You simply inhale deeply for a count of four, hold the breath for a count of four, exhale for four, and hold for four. Repeat. Repeat. Repeat.

I still use this technique and others I have learned to regulate my heart rate, and to ramp myself up or calm myself down, as the situation demands. It was also around this time that I first got my hands on a copy of *Meditations* by Marcus Aurelius. I recall Commander Wilson giving it to me, but I may be mistaken. I do know that later, when he served as the commanding officer of the Naval Special Warfare Center, he provided each new instructor with a copy. Regardless of where I got it, I never did return it. The copy of *Meditations* has stayed with me. It is worn and dog-eared, highlighted, underlined, and annotated. I reread it at least once per year, and recently had to break down and buy another copy.

Meditations was my first foray into the ideas of the Stoics. Much of it meshed with other warrior reading—from Miyamoto Masashi's *The Book of Five Rings*, Machiavelli's *The Prince*, Sun Tzu's *The Art of War*, and even Rudyard Kipling's poem "If," which got me though dive school. Today I owe much of my personal philosophy to the writings of these men and many others.

Often, on the way to a mission, I tried to focus on a piece of wisdom from Marcus Aurelius while I practiced box-breathing, especially his admonishments not to fear death. "Think of yourself as dead. You have lived your life. Now, take what's left, and live it properly." Or, "Do not act as if you were going to live ten thousand years. Death hangs over you. While you live, while it is in your power, be good."

As I understood Marcus's words, that meant being good at my job. Dedicated to honing my craft, and that perfection took the form of calculated risk and controlled chaos. The ability to flip the switch from deep breathing and quiet contemplation to unrelenting violence, inside the space of a heartbeat.

Every job during a mission is critical, but being on the assault team is where we all wanted to be. Mike was my breacher and was eminently competent. From the moment the vehicle glided to a halt, the team's job was to protect him as we moved to the breach point. His job might require cutting a fence, picking a lock, smashing a window, or blowing a door; and while intel usually gave some indication of what would be required, we all knew that things change, and on the move to the primary breach point he would have to take in all available information and make the call.

Mike and I in Najaf preparing to head out on another mission.

On June 8, we launched Objective Razor. On the outskirts of Baghdad, city blocks gave way to farmland, and paved roads to dirt canal trails not designed to withstand the weight of the armored Humvees. Our vehicles began to get stuck several hundred yards away from the target compound, three buildings surrounded by a thick mud wall.

The call came over the radio, "Hit it on foot." We dismounted and moved across the fields, entering the main opening of the compound. Each assault team peeled off to move to the breach point of their designated building. From the flat-topped roofs, heads poked up. We tossed flashbangs onto the roofs to keep them down. This far out in the country, doors were rarely locked and a breach was seldom necessary, so another flashbang went into the front room as we made entry.

The JTAC called in the helo from the loiter position to keep eyes on the rooftops as we cleared the buildings, taking stairs upward to access the doors to the roof. When the raid was complete, we detained fourteen fighting-aged males. The HUMINT guys gathered biometric data and worked to verify identities. Ultimately, twelve of the men were released. The two who were detained bore the distinct familial resemblance to the relatives of "X."

The interrogations took on the tone of a police procedural. While both men denied any wrongdoing, one fingered the other as the man we were looking for. The man suspected of being "X" was intelligent and refused to admit his identity. He sparred with interrogators and his calmness under questioning further convinced us that he was "X." Finally, after being confronted with the fact that multiple family members had identified him from a photo taken at the detention facility, he admitted his identity but refused to acknowledge any wrongdoing. He was an innocent bystander, caught up in war like everyone else, just trying to survive. With the IIG takeover looming, "X" would be tried in an Iraqi court, and to make a case against him he would either need to confess to the atrocities—bombings, and murders of coalition forces, as well as the Iraqi people—or we would have to provide solid proof.

So, our intel officer devised the kind of plan that someone always throws out and everyone says, "Yeah, that might work, but we could never get permission." Except this time, we had nothing to lose by asking. We asked and were granted authorization to give it a shot.

"X" knew, especially considering the recent Abu Ghraib scandal, that we wouldn't hurt him, but would he be so sure of his safety in the hands of the Kurds?

Major Kozeniesky reached out to Dr. Shaways, who agreed to help, so we coordinated a trip. I was back on the advance team. We drove ahead of the convoy to the Green Zone. I pulled into the small airfield and walked over to tower operations, housed in a raised trailer. An air force technical sergeant looked up from his desk.

"Hey man, you can't be in here."

"OK, but I need to tell someone that a C-130 is going to be landing here in twenty minutes, and when it does, I am going to need the rest of the field shut down while we drive two vehicles out to load up."

He glanced at the flight schedule posted on a whiteboard on the wall above his desk. "I'm not tracking a C-130 landing, and you're not allowed to take vehicles out on the runway."

"OK, but when the C-130 lands and you see vehicles driving out, that will be me. And it would be best if no other planes were landing at the time."

"How did you even get in here?"

I reached in my pocket and pulled out a red badge like the ones used by Ambassador Bremer's security detail. We had been issued the cards when we began the PSD. It was kind of cool, really—a flash of the card opened any door.

"Oh, shit. Can you have a seat here, and I'll check to see if I can find out about your C-130."

He returned a few minutes later, "Oh man, hey look, I'm sorry about that. We have your flight inbound. It will be on the ground any minute. Can I get a passenger manifest?"

"No, sorry, but there will be nine people boarding the aircraft." I raised my hand as a call came over the headset. "OK, my guys are here. Thanks."

I met them at the gate and then led the convoy across the tarmac to the waiting C-130, which had already turned around. They kept the engines running but lowered the ramp to allow our guys to board. Major Kozeniesky, Major Carter, and six shooters boarded the plane, escorting one hooded individual and Dr. Shaways. After they loaded, we drove off. As soon as we cleared the runway, the pitch of the engines changed, and the aircraft shot down the runway and lifted off.

I stopped back in the tower and said, "Hey guys, thanks for your help."

I regretted not being able to take the trip. The Marines that went described the area in the Erbil, Kurdistan region as a beautiful village near the foothills of the Zagros mountain range that borders Iran, with lush vegetation and smiling, friendly people. "Happy to see Americans" might have been debatable, but they were with Dr. Shaways, who was a hometown hero. The Marines tried to perform PSD functions, but Shaways wouldn't hear of it. "These are my people, I don't need to be protected here, and you don't need to carry your guns." They still carried their guns, but as ordered, enjoyed the hospitality and food provided by the villagers.

While they feasted, "X" was taken to a holding facility. He spoke enough English to get the gist of the conversation. He was being handed over to the Kurds, the Americans didn't care what happened to him anymore. They were returning to Baghdad.

"X" was led into a small damp room and handcuffed to a table. When his hood was removed and his eyes adjusted to the bright lights, he could make out, on the other side of the table, two stone-faced Kurdish men. They began asking questions.

"X" began talking. He was of course unaware that Majors Kozeniesky and Carter sat in chairs in the next room taking notes, or that the ruse was contingent on the Kurds' promise that no harm would come to "X" while in their charge. When the interrogation was complete, the group returned to Baghdad and "X" was passed off to coalition custody to await his day in court.

That was our last direct interaction with Dr. Shaways. He served his term as the IIG vice president and went on to serve three terms as the Deputy Prime Minister of Iraq between 2005 and 2015. He passed away in 2021. Years later, MARSOC Raiders would fight alongside the Kurdish Peshmerga in Syria. They were known to be brave fighters and a noble people.

As the IIG assumed control of Iraq, we returned our focus to those who wished to disrupt the fledgling government. The intel folks crossed "X" off the hierarchy and moved up the ladder to the other elusive target, "Z."

CHAPTER 12
THE ONE-ARMED MAN

We are the Pilgrims, master; we shall go
Always a little further; it may be
Beyond that last blue mountain barred with snow
Across that angry or that glimmering sea.
—James Elroy Flecker

I'm often asked, "What is the most important attribute for success in special operations?" In a way, it is a trick question. The attribute needed at the time is the most important. Smarts, speed, shooting ability, teamwork, or interpersonal skills are crucial at certain times and they can make or break a mission. But my answer is always the same: mental toughness. You may know it by other names: grit, resilience, fortitude, or perseverance. You can find countless YouTube videos promising secrets, programs, and plans to build mental toughness. But the real secret is simple.

Do hard things and don't quit.

The best teacher is the acceptance born of necessity. I imagine humans can learn to accept anything, given enough repetitions and too few options. At the most basic level, it is simply a matter choosing to fight for life over curling up in a ball and waiting for death.

I've seen the starving fight for scraps, the refugees make homes amid rubble, the poor perform any task that will pay enough to allow them to make it until tomorrow...because the other option is unthinkable.

For us, mental toughness was a part of the job, and the best teacher is deprivation and scarcity of options. In a firefight you can freeze, flee, or fight. Only one option addresses the problem, the other two delay an inevitable outcome.

And deprivation comes with blessings. If you sleep enough nights on rocky ground, the thinnest mattress becomes a luxury, so like recovering alcoholics and the Stoics, we learned to accept the things we couldn't change. But instead of just accepting them, we chose to relish them—to look at hardship and privation as an investment in some future indulgence, even if that indulgence was only a hot cup of bad coffee, a water bottle shower on a hot day, or a warm beer after a mission.

It's harder to build mental toughness when there are choices, or when you can just pick up your ball and go home. You need to find ways to limit options. Put on a ruck and walk farther from home than you think wise, and leave no choice but to make it back. Swim out in the ocean farther than you ever have. Yes, that may be dangerous advice, but toughness can't be developed in the comfort zone. You need to narrow focus to a binary choice: swim or die. Do hard things and accept no result but success. At every opportunity, push yourself beyond what you thought possible.

The military in general, but special operations specifically, breeds mental toughness because the life provides the perfect petri dish for it to grow. Possibly the most valuable lesson that I learned during my career was to dig the well of mental toughness deep enough so that you will always be able to draw from it. And after a time, you begin to *need* to draw from it, and you learn to find a perverse pleasure in enduring.

There is a quote I first saw on a poster taped to the wall of a bar in the town of Kin on my first deployment to Okinawa, Japan many years ago that read in part, "the best times of my life were times that others would say were best forgotten." That quote always returns to me at the worst of times and makes them somehow more bearable. For those of us in the Det, it was our commitment to the gospel of strong backs and hard feet that drove out the demons of quit, and that made tough times the times we cherished.

It is the same with mortar and rocket fire. After a time, it becomes background noise, like living near the train tracks with intermittent explosions. You've got to live your life, move about, do all the things that need doing, while burying the idea floating in the back of your head that at any moment you might be turned into a crater.

Honestly, we didn't have it as bad as a lot of places, but for a time during the summer it got worse. The attacks usually came in the afternoon or early evening, when they knew we were up and moving around. On one occasion I heard the thump from a mortar launch when we were outside working out, but usually it was the high-pitched whine that announced incoming. It seemed to originate from nowhere, somewhere above us. If you heard the whine, it meant the rounds were going long. Usually they went long, exploding in the wooded area beyond Camp Mylar, or in the large open field between us and Fifth Group's compound. If you were inside, you probably didn't even hear the whine, just the thud of the explosion. Usually, it was one single rocket, or two to three mortar rounds in rapid succession, fired from a hastily established firing position by nervous insurgents with little skill in aiming. The tube or launcher was pulled from a car trunk or the bed of a pickup, quickly pointed and fired, then the perpetrators loaded up the hot barrel and sped off before they could be discovered.

One morning they got lucky. Formations are often the bane of military life, time spent standing around waiting for someone of greater rank to come out and say something. But there are times when they are warranted. We seldom held formations in combat, but on this day, someone was being promoted, and we were glad to be there to witness the event. Since we were already awake and dressed, a few of us planned to drive over to the chow hall at Camp Liberty to grab lunch for a change of pace, and our body armor and helmets sat in the vehicles waiting for us. And so there we were, standing in neat rows in the heat when the whistle came overhead. The formation dissipated as each man ran for the nearest cover, some to various buildings, others crouched behind barriers or vehicles for protection from flying shrapnel.

The rounds landed in a succession of thumps, crashing out over our heads harmlessly. Then one landed close, just beyond the row of palm trees that lined the road between our buildings and the JOC. The round impacted like a sledgehammer on a tin roof, and the concussive force of overpressure was strong enough to be felt in my back teeth. A plume of smoke rose in front of the JOC.

The formation was forgotten. The promotion would be awarded without ceremony at some convenient time. We raced toward the JOC. Parked in front of the building, Commander Wilson's white pickup truck sat, glass shattered, metal torn. The round had landed squarely in the truck's bed. Wilson and the master chief, his senior enlisted advisor, had just returned from a meeting. Commander Wilson had gone into the JOC while the master chief lingered outside when the attack began. The blood trail led from the truck up the white concrete steps into the vestibule of the JOC, where he collapsed.

The corpsmen jumped into action, monitoring his breathing, cutting open clothing with shears to find and stem bleeding from shrapnel wounds, and wrapping them in dressings. They treated for the hypovolemic shock caused by blood loss. It was amazing to watch them work.

While we all receive a good bit of training in tactical combat casualty care, the Marine Corps does not possess its own medical personnel. We borrow from the navy. Of the thousands of navy corpsmen, only very few are qualified as SARCs, Special Amphibious Reconnaissance Corpsmen. These men complete all of the same tactical training that Marine special operators do, but in addition, they spend nearly a year learning combat-trauma lifesaving and are often assigned to ply their skills in high-risk emergency rooms and shock-trauma wards. They are some of the best men I have ever known, and they all go by "Doc."

They spoke to each other in calm, clear voices.

"Distal pulse strong but thready."

"Have we got all bleeders stopped?"

"This side's good. Help me roll him."

Without taking his eyes off the patient, Doc asked, "How far out is the medevac?"

"Five minutes out."

"Right, let's get him packaged. I'll go with him. Is the vehicle ready?"

"It's waiting outside."

"Get the backboard under him. I need bodies to carry."

"We've got four."

"Hey, Master Chief, you're doing good. We're going to lift you and get you out of here. Stay with me. How are you doing?" The measured way they spoke to the master chief was meant to calm and reassure as much as to keep him alert and conscious. As we carried him out, a young sailor stood with towels ready to clean up the mess.

The medevac helo landed in the zone just two hundred meters from the JOC. In a minute, the master chief was loaded, and the helo lifted off. He would make a full recovery, but the fact that the nuisance of mortars and rockets had hurt one of us pissed us off. We began brainstorming ways to eliminate the mortars and rocket teams.

One attempt to deal with the issue involved an elaborate ruse dubbed Operation Serpent Strike, which was initiated by soldiers from the Second Battalion, Fifth Special Forces Group. They contracted a group of Iraqi workers to construct a stage in a large open field just west of Camp Myler. It was apparent that the stage was going to be used for some important function. The soldiers who were keeping an eye on the workers let slip random bits of information about the size and importance of the event, and we made sure that it was known that the stage needed to be completed by a certain date. The hope was that word of the planned event would filter back to the insurgents, and that they would view it as an opportunity that would be too good to pass up.

When the designated date arrived, no Iraqis were permitted on the camp that could potentially get word out that the planned gathering was not happening.

Aircraft circled high overhead looking for signs of a launch, and a local artillery unit had diverted its counter-battery radar to cover the area and hopefully identify the launch point. We sat sweating, jocked up in our vehicles, ready to storm out of the gate and speed to any identified launch site. As evening came, we sat begging for a launch, hoping for the opportunity for retribution, just wanting to do something. When the sun sank without an attack, we opened the gates anyway and headed out to several locations that had been identified through a source. The GROM hit several targets, and we hit others. The locations all showed signs of having been used as launch sites—scorched marks on the ground and indentations from mortar baseplates— but no activity or weapons caches. Disappointed, we returned home.

We started manning a sniper position high in the tower of the pink hotel across the street from Camp Myler. After spending all night out on raids, we would return to climb the endless stairwells to a vantage point just below the roof. In two-man sniper teams, we took shifts using binoculars to glass the open fields, watching farmers at work spending the day toiling under the impassive sun. Children played in dust lots and splashed and floated boats in the irrigation canals.

As a unit, we had a very high percentage of trained snipers. I had the benefit of being assigned to a sniper platoon very early in my career and had served as an instructor, so Colonel Coates had given me oversight of our sniper training and weapons. We brought with us our regular complement of USMC sniper weapons, including the M40A3, a 7.62 bolt-action sniper rifle built from a Remington 700 chassis. This rifle had been the workhorse of the USMC sniper, with few modifications since Vietnam, and was accurate out to around one thousand yards.

The Marine Corps also issued the Barrett M82 SASR, or Special Application Scoped Rifle. The SASR fired a massive .50 caliber BMG round. While it lacked the precision of a sniper rifle, it was accurate enough for most work out to and over one thousand meters. It also fired the Norwegian-made Raufoss round, which is a high-explosive, incendiary, armor-piercing projectile that is incredibly effective against vehicles and hard targets. In Norwegian, Raufoss means "red waterfall." I always believed it to be an incredibly cruel name derived from the round's effects on the human body, but only recently learned that it was named for the town it is produced in, which in turn is named for a nearby river that appears red because of the high iron content.

Fortunately, because we were given authorization to conduct research and development, we also brought along the MK11 sniper rifle, a semi-automatic rifle that would see the most use. Because it looked very similar to the M4s we carried, our snipers were better able to blend in. Being seen carrying a sniper rifle is a sure way to draw fire.

And while the real precision range of the MK11 was probably about eight hundred meters, in built-up urban areas that was usually more than adequate.

The final sniper weapon in our arsenal was the CheyTac .408 Intervention rifle. As far as I know, we were the first unit to take this weapon to combat. Shortly before our deployment, Sid, Vinnie, and I accompanied Jon Laplume to the Shooters, Hunters and Outdoor Trade Show, or SHOT, in Las Vegas. It is the industry trade show for all things weapons. While there, we met a fellow named Todd Hodnett. He was working to expand the concept of long-range precision by combining the CheyTac with a scope-and-ballistic software from a company called Horus Vision. They had developed a new scope reticle system, and a ballistic software computer to assist with the myriad calculations necessary to achieve real precision at distances over one mile.

Todd offered to come out to Camp Pendleton and give us a demonstration. In USMC circles, questioning the Unertl scope that had been in use since World War II was akin to blasphemy. But we were looking for any advantage that we could get, and after a few days of shooting with Todd, we were sold. We were able to purchase two CheyTacs and enough ammo to keep them fed. If we had observed a mortar team setting up, the CheyTac would have been the perfect weapon at the ranges we expected, but the hours in the sniper position netted nothing but lost sleep.

Mike later carried the CheyTac into An Najaf, and used it to deal with a knucklehead who was shooting at us from behind a dumpster several blocks away. But the weapon was too large and unwieldy for street-to-street fighting, and the buildings limited the range that we could observe, rendering the weapon relatively useless.

By this point in the deployment, our HUMINT guys had been developing their own sources—Iraqis who, for a variety of reasons, offered their services as informants. One of Scotty's sources provided information on a local rocket cell that had been responsible for several attacks in the local area and may have been involved in the master chief's injury.

Scotty gave the source a vehicle to use and a simple Global Positioning System, and taught him how to mark positions. He was able to return with the identified locations of three launch points. Several days later he returned with photographs of the launch sites. With this information, the intel folks were able to pinpoint a target, a welder who was producing rocket launchers. When asked how we could positively identify the target, the source replied, "It will be easy, he only has one arm."

At 2:20 a.m. on July 27, we launched Objective Relapse. The plan called for three simultaneous hits. We would conduct two, and the GROM would hit the third target. We were focused on the ringleader. The man we had dubbed "The One-Armed Bandit."

It was a rural target outside of Baghdad. We drove along dirt roads flanking fields of wheat and barley. At intervals, deep, large irrigation trenches ran alongside fields, and the road surface served as a levee. The trenches were filled by diverting water from the Tigris and Euphrates in a method called flood irrigation, making possible the crops that grow in the otherwise arid soil. The size and weight of our vehicles made the driving treacherous, especially on our NODs. Often, portions of the road surface would collapse beneath our wheels. For this reason, and because of the fear of IEDs laid in our wake, we never returned the same way we came.

It was a dark night. The moon was hidden behind heavy cloud cover. At a levee junction several hundred meters from the targets, the assault force dismounted. I proceeded with Eric up a levee, to provide containment of the objective. He and I positioned ourselves along the levee. A wide irrigation ditch separated us from the objective. From my position I could make out the glow of the infrared flags each man wore for identification, bobbing through the wheat. Above our heads, too high to be heard, an AC-130 gunship circled. Random reports crackled through my headset.

Before the assaulters even got close, an urgent call came into my headset. "We've got squirters!"

Two "squirters" fled through the back door of the compound, separated, and began running through the wheat fields. It's likely that they had been tipped off by a phone call. Each small town that we drove through played some part in the insurgent early warning network. The closer we got to an objective, the more the watchers were able to narrow down the target and provide early warning.

When the situation allowed, we would employ a Blackhawk helicopter with a few shooters that could serve the role of aerial snipers/squirter control to mitigate this risk. But tonight, because we were hitting multiple objectives, we didn't have the men to spare.

I keyed my headset and flipped on the small IR beacon taped to the top of my helmet.

"Spooky, this is 4-1. I'm activating my IR strobe on the levee, west of the objective. Do you tally?"

"4-1, tally your strobe. You have one squirter moving your way on the far side of the canal."

"Roger, solid copy, keep an eye on him." Switching nets, I put out an open call. "Is anyone going after the west-side squirter?"

"Negative, 4-1, he's yours."

"Roger." I turned to Eric. "Hold down the fort here. I'm going swimming."

"Do you want me to go? You're pretty short." My height (a perfectly normal five foot seven) often made me the butt of jokes.

"Fuck off. I could use a bath anyway. Plus, how deep can it be?"

Pretty deep, as it turned out. It was also not really water but a thick, viscous sludge. I thought I would be able to slide in holding my rifle overheard to keep it dry, and I assumed the depth would allow me to wade across. The sloped sides of the ditch were slick clay. When I stepped to the edge, my feet went out from under me, so I leapt in in a bid to retain my balance. The ditch was deep enough that while I fully submerged, I did not touch bottom. Scissor-kicking to get my head and rifle above the muck, I began the began the long process of side-stroking across a canal filled with who knew what. I managed to keep it mostly out of my mouth. Although it wasn't terribly wide, with body armor, ammo, radios, and basic Line 1 equipment, I was gassed by the time I made it. I could tell that Eric was stifling a laugh at my expense. Then I had to contend with the slick mud again as I fought to pull myself out onto the far side.

As I lay panting in the wheat, my radio crackled. It was Chunks. "4-1, 2-1—I'm headed your way, after the squirter."

"Shit." I wished I'd gotten that call a minute ago—I'd be dry. But I radioed back, "Roger, I'm between you and him, moving your way."

I pulled myself up, cleared my rifle, and hoping the barrel wasn't too full of slop to shoot, if needed, I stepped out into the wheat field.

The gunship was able to vector us in on the squirter, who had gone to ground. They could identify the silhouette of his heat signature amid the waist-high wheat.

Chunks and I made contact and moved on parallel routes separated by ten meters. Approaching a squirter is a dangerous time. You don't know if he is armed or wearing a body bomb and was just waiting to take one of us out with him.

I could hear from the chatter on the radio that the buildings were secure, and the search was commencing, but they hadn't located "Jackpot."

"He's directly between you two, ten meters ahead."

I couldn't hear Chunks moving forward, but I knew he was. We moved in a crouch, the wheat swaying green through our NODs. Then I caught a flash of a white dishdasha. He was lying prone, trying to hide. I brought up my weapon and heard Chunks call out, "Arni yadayk!" Show me your hands!

The form tried to sink deeper into the dry ground. I pressed the switch that turned on my weapon-mounted light. "Get up, put your hands up!"

He struggled to his knees and when he raised his arms, the right sleeve of his dishdasha hung empty.

Chunks pressed the mike and called out, "We've got Jackpot. Bringing him in." He escorted the one-armed bandit back to the objective and reunited him with his prosthetic arm. I took a long walk around to find a bridge to cross, to link back up with Eric.

During site exploitation, the team recovered detailed maps of Baghdad area military bases, with annotations indicating times and locations most susceptible to attack.

On their objective, the GROM recovered ten rocket launchers with weapons sights, among other items.

During the drive back, there were loud complaints about how I smelled. When we returned to Camp Myler, I got hosed down, then Doc promptly administered a shot of gamma globulin (which is like receiving an injection of chunky peanut butter) in my left ass cheek, to ward off infection from any of the myriad contaminants in the water.

Then, while everyone else went to sleep, I got to spend hours fully disassembling my weapons, scrubbing the mud away with a toothbrush, then digging caked-on crud from the nooks and crannies with repurposed dental tools, before lubricating and reassembling and test-firing my rifle, pistol, and breaching gun.

CHAPTER 13

CITY OF THE DEAD

*There, between the city of the dead and the city of the
living, I meditated. I thought of the eternal silence
in the first and the endless sorrow in the second.*
—Khalil Gabran

We had returned home from another late-night raid outside of the
city. Detainees we handed off, weapons and vehicles we cleaned,
and equipment we reloaded, inspected, and staged. Now the sun was
rising, and my night's work was done. I wanted breakfast, then bed.

I was well into a plate of scrambled eggs and overcooked bacon
when Captain Thompson pulled up a chair, sat down across from me,
and asked, "Ranger, what do you know about Najaf?"

I knew a little. Before coming to Iraq, I had read about the country
and its history. Najaf was famous for its mosque. Legends tell that in
661 CE, Ali ibn Abi Talib—cousin and brother-in-law of the Prophet
Muhammad, and the last Rashidun caliph of Islam, mentioned earlier—was wounded by an assassin with a poisoned sword. Before he
died, he instructed his followers to tie him to the back of a white camel
and let it wander freely. Where it stopped, they were to bury him.
Where it stopped, became Najaf. The Imam Ali Mosque and its compound grew around it.

More recently, the Grand Ayatollah Muhammad Muhammad
Sadeq al-Sadr, an outspoken opponent of Saddam Hussein's Ba'athist

government, was assassinated there in 1999. Two of his sons were also killed. Saddam's government denied responsibility.

The US Army secured Najaf during the 2003 invasion, later turning it over to the Iraqi Army. Eighteen months later, Najaf was in the intel reports again. One of al-Sadr's surviving sons, Muqtada al-Sadr, was now the leader of the Mahdi Army. His forces had seized the city with seven thousand fighters, headquartered in the mosque. A multinational task force had Najaf surrounded, waiting for special-ops teams to infiltrate the city to observe, report, and eliminate as many insurgents as possible. If we could force Sadr's men to retreat into the mosque complex, coalition forces could move in unimpeded, reducing casualties.

"When do they want us there?" I asked.

"You're already late," he said as he stood. "You can sleep when you're dead."

Even under the circumstances, I was excited to visit Najaf, a place with such history. Our seven-man team packed what we needed: sniper rifles, ammo, radios, and food. We planned a route, loaded our armored Humvees, and drove southwest on Highway Eight out of Baghdad. We broke off near Hillah, continuing on Highway Seventy through the fertile farmlands bordering the Euphrates, where waist-high wheat plants swayed in the breeze, boys drove herds of cattle and sheep, and goats stood munching grass, looking completely unimpressed by our mounted machine guns. The irrigated land was so green it was almost possible to forget where we were and why, until we had to detour bomb-damaged bridges or skirt towns where ambush was likely.

That evening we arrived at the old schoolhouse where Task Force Cougar was headquartered. The commander welcomed us and used a map to point out key locations, showing where the friendly and enemy forces were. The biggest concern was the mosque. The United States couldn't be responsible for damaging it, so there were limits to where the task force could go and what weapons could be used. The Law of Armed Conflict protects holy sites. Placing an army inside a holy site negates much of that distinction, but in this case the mosque was more than just a mosque. The Imam Ali Mosque is the third holiest site for Shia Muslims. The commander used his finger to trace a circle, drawn in grease pencil, on the map. It established a border, well outside of the mosque walls, as his limit of advance. But our rules of engagement were different. We weren't under the same restrictions, but once we crossed that line, we were on our own.

A convoy of trucks arrived, carrying dinner. We ate what would be our last hot meal for days: fatty pork cutlets, cold green beans, mushy carrot medallions, and sticky white rice, served on sagging plates made of recycled paper. The Vikings had mead before battle; we had cherry Kool-Aid and lukewarm, bitter coffee from big steel vats, in Styrofoam cups.

We all found a spot to sit cross-legged in the dirt and balance our plates on knees or laps. I talked with a young soldier. Many of the young men around us were visibly nervous about the potential fight to come. I noticed one of our guys, Glen, hurriedly finish eating and move into the building. Glen was not only a fantastic sniper who I had served with in Afghanistan, but also someone who could be counted on to liven the mood when needed. I suspected he was up to something and kept my eyes on the door. He is a big guy, dark-complected with jet-black hair. Two minutes later, the door flew open, and he came running out dressed in a dirty, white Arabic dishdasha, what we called a "man dress." His hands were raised above his head in surrender. He was babbling in an incoherent language. All of our guys broke down laughing, but we noticed several of the young soldiers grasp for their weapons. We quickly put a stop to the fun.

After Glen's performance, we finished dinner, then returned to planning and preparing. I went over the route with my point man, Mike, while the others re-checked radios and cleaned weapons. I told them to get some sleep.

I couldn't. I went over the map again, committing the route to memory. At midnight, I woke them. Our ride, a patrol made up of four Bradley Fighting Vehicles, was getting ready to head out. Another team leader, Terry, would remain with the HQ to help coordinate our operations with those of the other SOF sniper teams operating in the city. Over the course of the mission, he kept us informed of what was happening around us, and we passed to friendly forces information that he relayed on enemy movement.

At the gate to the compound, a line of Bradleys sat waiting for us, engines rumbling, soldiers scrambling around and over them, completing pre-combat checks and pre-combat inspections, which we just called PCCs and PCIs. As we approached, a young-looking sergeant greeted us and directed us to our vehicle.

I hated riding in the back of armored vehicles. It was like being shut in a metal tomb—protective but close, claustrophobic. No sense of my surroundings, no idea where I was, no longer in charge of my own destiny. Expecting any moment to hear—or not hear—an IED tear through the armor. Strangely, those were the times when I was most afraid. It's hard to pretend to be immortal when your life is in someone else's hands.

The air in the Bradley was stale and sour with the smell of sweat we'd become accustomed to; the tight quarters reminded us of our filth. The noise was ceaseless, even under the communications headset I wore. The tracks of the vehicle grated against the roadway, and the grinding drone of the engine vibrated the thick steel of the vehicle's hull, a constant rumble felt bone-deep. We rode wearing our heavy packs, which pressed against the hull, forcing us to the edge of the narrow bench seats. I was bent forward at the waist until my helmet almost touched Mike's, who was sitting across from me. My rifle was between my legs, the stock resting on the toe of my boot to protect it from the jarring, my arms wrapped around the scope. It wasn't a long trip, twenty blocks maybe, but it took forever.

Finally, I heard over my headset, "End of the next block's your drop-off."

Our night was just beginning. Soldiers from another vehicle exited first and took up positions to provide security. The back hatch of our vehicle opened, letting the night air in, and us out. A Bradley crewman kneeling by the ramp pulled his headphones away from his ear when I bent toward him, my mouth close to him. "Thanks, Sergeant. Y'all take it easy. Make sure you're listening up for the next half hour, in case things go south. If we need a quick extract, we'll fight our way back to this corner."

He gave me a thumbs-up and shut the hatch. We waited as they loaded back up and drove off, turning the corner. The noise faded. We were alone.

I nodded to Mike, and he stood and moved. At intervals, each man rose and followed. Navigation was simple—just head toward the giant golden dome. The streets were empty. The whole city felt deserted, except for a few starving dogs. In the coming days they'd feast, and die, but for now, they massed and lurked in the shadows at the edge of our sight, waiting for someone to fall.

The cobblestone streets were worn smooth by one thousand years of foot traffic. There were no sidewalks; the road extended up to houses and storefronts. No lights shone except those illuminating the mosque. Above our heads, an electrician's nightmare: a spiderweb of power lines and wires and cables, spliced and taped and feeding into windows and power boxes. Some drooped almost to head level.

The smell was familiar: a mixture of cooking spices and feces and soot and rotting things, no different than a Manila slum, a Bangkok alley, or a Tijuana side street. Not bad really, but distinctive. I'd spent much of my adult life in places like this. The windows were covered in metal grates; the doors made of heavy wood or welded steel, secured with thick padlocks, as the occupants fled ahead of the coming fight. Through the night-vision goggles hanging from my helmet, the cityscape glowed in mottled shades of green.

I knelt at the corner of two nameless streets. My eyes and rifle pointed down the road to the left, looking for shine, or movement. I used the building to cover most of my body, exposing as little as possible as I scanned the shadows. We bounded this way, each man taking turns crossing the intersection and picking up security. No words needed. A tap on my back by a passing teammate told me I was now the last man. The far corner was covered. I didn't need to check. I rose to a half-crouch and moved, head, eyes, and rifle pointing left. We wore assault boots—more sneaker than boot—the rubber soles silent against the stone.

We moved from shadow to shadow, heads on swivels, turning to point the muzzle of our rifles into open windows or ducking beneath them as we passed. Up seven blocks and turn left. Two more blocks to the building we had picked out from overhead photos. It was a hotel or apartment building, deserted now. No people, little furniture, no running water, but seven stories high, and height is advantage. Height lets you see deeper into recesses, blind alleys. The building was less than five hundred yards from the mosque's outer wall. Our sniper rifles were accurate to twice that distance.

We cleared the building methodically in two-man teams, covering each floor, entering each room, finally occupying the top floor. Then we tackled our priorities of work: security, communications, and observation. We placed old cans and glass on the landings below. A simple but effective early-warning device; anyone entering would make enough noise to notify our sentry. I set the schedule for watch on the only stairwell, covered the contingencies one more time, and assigned responsibilities. Then Mike and I moved to the roof.

The roof was cooler. I stripped off my body armor. A light breeze from the west chilled my sweat-soaked torso, even though the temperature was still in the eighties. Mike crawled across to the edge of the roof to photograph the area and survey our position. His photographs would be transmitted by satellite back to Baghdad, where they would give commanders a near-real-time look at the situation. I knelt, extending the metal bipod legs of my rifle until they clicked into place. The flat roof was coated with gravel-covered tar paper. I cursed myself for not bringing elbow pads. A wall, a foot or so high, circled the roof. It was enough to provide cover. At regular intervals, drain holes opened on the city, maybe twelve-by-six inches. Enough to see through. Enough to shoot through. I picked a spot alongside an elevator maintenance room to set up my position. It would keep us in shadow and hopefully give us some shade as the sun rose. Once prepared, there was time to wait. I sat cross-legged beside my rifle and looked out on the city.

The Imam Ali Mosque occupied the view to my front. The dome was covered by 7,777 gold-plated tiles, glowing in the ambient light.

Against the pinkening sky, it was an illustration from an old copy of *Arabian Nights*.

To my left, in the waning moonlight, I could just see the shadows of the Wadi al-Salam cemetery, "The Valley of Peace"—the irony wasn't lost on anyone. Wadi al-Salam is the largest cemetery in the world, five million bodies within its tombs and crypts. According to custom, the dead were to be buried there before the next sunset. The bodies would have been washed and wrapped in a white cotton shroud, then taken to the Imam Ali shrine and carried three times around the tomb. Finally, they would have been taken to the Wadi al-Salam and placed in a prepared grave, while a cleric recited verses from the Koran.

I hoped the dead would be given proper burials, but in the days to come there were going to be so many.

Scanning right, I paused at the golden minarets. They looked like rooks on the off-kilter chessboard of the city, the game paused on account of darkness. Soon it would resume, and pawns would be sacrificed. But for those few tranquil moments, I was awed to witness the juncture between ancient history and modern warfare.

I was there—in Najaf that day—because seventeen years before, just a couple of weeks out of high school, I joined the Marines. More out of a sense of adventure than patriotism. I wanted to get away from my little West Virginia town and its factory jobs. I hadn't had a bad childhood, just not the one I wanted. I wanted to see the world. I wanted something more. I found a home in the Marine Corps. I was good at the job and loved the excitement.

But now I had a family to think about. The ones I couldn't write death letters to. They were why I needed to be immortal. I also had the men with me. We looked out for each other, but I was in charge, responsible for them and to their families for returning them home safe. Another weight that sits heavy.

A pouch on my vest held an Iridium satellite phone with a large antenna that folded out and extended. Another means of communicating with headquarters. I thought about calling Tracy to describe what I was seeing, but pushed the thought from my head. On missions, I tried not to think of home. It wasn't helpful. Thinking of home can make you cautious, tentative when decisiveness is called for. Hesitation is one of many things that can kill.

Mike crawled back over, took a seat beside me, and rested the Canon camera in his lap. "I got some good pictures of the city."

"We'll send them later," I said. "Make sure you save copies. They'll make great Christmas cards."

"Probably be our only souvenirs of this place," he said, with a half-smile.

"Yeah, I doubt the mosque gift shop is open."

"Well, I forgot my wallet anyway," he finished, and turned back to his camera.

As the sun rose, it was time to work. I wet a bandanna with a mouthful of water from a Nalgene bottle, then spread it out under the muzzle of my sniper rifle, to absorb the dust that would kick up when I fired. A dust cloud could give away our position to anyone looking. I lay behind the MK11, covered my head with a thin mesh net, and ran the edge out over the scope, to keep the rising sun from glinting off the glass. I slid my face down the stock until my cheekbone was firmly seated in the familiar spot. My right hand found the pistol grip, trigger finger extended along the rolled metal lip of the magazine well. I wouldn't touch the trigger until I needed to. My thumb felt for the safety and confirmed it was on. I bent my left arm at the elbow, made a fist, and tucked it in the pocket of my right shoulder, under the butt of the rifle. I lay as flat as I could get, legs straight behind me, the heels of my feet turned inward like a ballerina. Mike lay to my left, talking to the guys downstairs on the radio, relaying to them what we were seeing.

The sun peeked from the east; the first rays reflected off the golden dome. It began to gleam like a second, closer sun, until I couldn't look at it through my scope. The light stretched out, illuminating the cemetery, shadows growing like a many-fingered hand taking the city in its grasp. It was quiet—and then it got quieter. Silence, as if the city itself had sucked in its breath and now held it; we were all in a vacuum. Then it began, the Adhan, the Shia call to prayer. Blaring from loudspeakers atop the minarets, loud and tinny, so close:

*Allah u Akbar Allah u Akbar Allah u Akbar Allah u
Akbar Ash-hadu alla ilaha illallah*

*Ash-hadu alla ilaha illallah Ash-hadu anna Muhammadan
rasulullah Ash-hadu anna*

*Muhammadan rasulullah Ash-hadu anna Aliya wali-ul-
lah Ash-hadu anna Aliya wali-ullah Hayya 'alas-salat
Hayya 'alas-salat Hayya 'alal-falah Hayya 'alal-falah
Hayya-al Khair al amal Hayya-al Khair al amal Allah
u Akbar Allah u Akbar La ilaha illallah La ilaha illallah*

Normally, I closed my eyes in deference; but that day, I scanned through my scope, looking for movement, determining distances, reading the wind, the light. The Adhan ended, and quiet returned for a moment. Then life began again; dogs barked, random noises echoed along empty urban canyons.

Then movement in the twisted streets between our position and the mosque walls. I saw the old man first. He walked straight to a small, white plastic table and righted a chair that lay on its side. He sat at what had been a corner cafe. I imagined better times. Tables of old men with pots of hot tea and bread or pastries, sticky with honey. They would talk and watch the young men and women off to work or to market, the children off to school, and the smaller children barefoot, playing in the dirty street. I wish I could have been there then, to join them for a cup of sweet, hot, mint tea—to ask five hundred questions about the town, the mosque, the cemetery, their lives, and the lives of their ancestors. But there weren't any noncombatants left in the city, and there was no room for sentiment here.

The old man was bald, smoking; he carried no weapon but had an air of authority. He was joined by another man, who deferred to him. This one middle-aged, with an AK-47 slung over one shoulder and a bottle of water. He sat, poured water into his hands, and ran them over his face and through his thick dark hair, slicking it back. They talked, heads close together.

157

Then he rounded the corner. He was young, but what we called a Military-Aged Male. Probably no older than I was when I left West Virginia. He had dark, uncombed hair and a thin beard, patchy across his cheeks. An attempt to make himself look older. But he carried a machine gun. AKs were a dinar a dozen. But he had an RPK light machine gun. They didn't just hand those out. He must have been trusted, despite his age. He was vigilant, keeping watch while the others talked.

I could have taken out the old man. He was important. He might even have reported to Sadr. I could have taken his comrade with the wet hair, probably a lower-level leader. But the young man was the easiest target, and his weapon was the greatest threat. If I took him first, maybe I could get the others before they stood, and if not, I'd be sending a message that would resonate inside the mosque walls. *There is nowhere in Najaf where your men are safe.*

The distance was just under three hundred yards. Smoke from the old man's cigarette drifted toward the boy. Telling me the wind was negligible, out of the west at three miles per hour. I twisted the eyepiece of my scope to increase the magnification and watched. Brown eyes. A loose tan tunic called a kurta, worn over dark trousers. The RPK on a sling over his left shoulder.

I pressed forward with my right thumb, taking off the safety. My finger bent into the trigger guard, slipping across the smooth metal until the joint of the first knuckle touched its edge. The trigger rested under the pad of my finger. The gravel dug into my elbows.

My crosshairs settled on his face. His brown eyes were untroubled. I could make a headshot at that range, but the head is too animated; the old man could call out to him, and he would turn. My heart was beating faster and harder than I liked. With each thump of my chest, he jumped in my scope.

I closed my eyes and inhaled through my nose, pulling air deep into my abdomen, a habit I developed long ago. I opened them as I exhaled, slowly. I tried to slow my heart through force of will. I moved the crosshairs to the second button of his kurta. Time slowed. It got quiet again, but now the quiet was in my head. I couldn't hear anything around me, just blood pumping. I could feel each heartbeat in my ears, a deep bass-drum thump. My vision tunneled. I couldn't see anything outside of his silhouette in the scope. I'd done this thousands of times before in training, on sniper ranges shooting at paper targets in the shape of men. It's the same thing, I told myself. One more breath. I let it out, and during the natural respiratory pause, I squeezed the trigger.

The sear released and the hammer was driven forward, striking the firing pin, which punctured the primer, which initiated a chain reaction. A small spark ignited the gunpowder. The rapid conversion from solid to gas caused pressure to build. The only way to relieve it was to drive the projectile into the barrel, where it began to spin, increasing stability and accuracy. The projectile exited the barrel at 2,571 feet per second. The suppressor trapped the gas, directing it through a series of metal baffles that dampen the sound.

He didn't hear the shot that killed him.

Less than a quarter-second later the bullet hit, level with his nipples, a hair left of center. It penetrated the breastbone and lungs and pulled bone fragments with it. His heart shredded with the impact. The projectile flipping, shedding pieces of its copper jacket as it mushroomed, tumbling through muscle, fat, tissue, and bone, severing the lower cervical spine on exit. His brown eyes didn't register recognition. His arms reached outward, looking for something to grab, fingers extended. His legs straightened for a second and then, like a baby learning to walk, he sat backward and fell. He sat there upright, legs stretched in front of him, arms still reaching, trying to breathe through shattered lungs. Frothy blood bubbled from his mouth and ran into his beard and onto his kurta. He slumped left, rolled flat on his back, the machine gun by his side. His brown eyes didn't quite close.

I realized I was still holding my breath. I blew out, then gulped air in. In, out—trying to regain control of my pounding heart.

I had forgotten the other men. By the time I looked away from his body, they were gone, vanished down an alley into the maze of the city. The plastic chairs, toppled, and the water bottle lying on its side, dripping onto the cobblestone. The body was left in the street.

It was hard to look away, like breaking a connection, but I had to return to work, scanning the area. I took several more shots from the roof before someone figured out where we were and found a vantage point to engage us. Mike and I sprinted back into the protection of the building under machine-gun fire from an adjacent rooftop.

I didn't see him again after that; I couldn't find the spot where he'd fallen. I've wondered what happened to the body. Most were left to lie in the sun until darkness fell. Nighttime provided some protection for those who pulled the bodies from the street.

I wouldn't have let one of my guys lie there; that was a promise we made to one another. We would have massed firepower, launched rockets, called in helicopter gunships, and sent a team to recover our dead. We had seen bodies in the street. Seen what the dogs did. My guys would shoot the dogs. I didn't stop them, but I couldn't do it. They were just trying to survive, too.

***

We spent another week in Najaf, moving each night to set up in a new location. Each day tightening the noose. I looked at a lot of faces through my scope. I killed more men. I didn't keep count. Their faces didn't stick with me like his did. Whether it was because he was young, or the first I had killed that way, I don't know. I had, and still have, his blood and the others' blood equally on my hands. It stains, but I've found the stains wear lighter with time.

I don't know if anyone is sure why al-Sadr took Najaf, or what he wanted, or what he thought would happen. Maybe he just wanted to thumb his nose at the Iraqi government and the Americans. Maybe he thought he would die a martyr, like his father and brothers, or maybe he knew we wouldn't risk damaging the mosque. Maybe he got what he wanted all along. On August 27, the Ayatollah Sistani negotiated a withdrawal with the Iraqi government. What was left of the Mahdi army stacked their weapons in the courtyard of the mosque and walked, unchallenged, through the cemetery into the desert. None of it meant anything.

We returned to the army command post outside of town to debrief, clean up, and await our helo back to camp Myler. Just before we moved out to the landing zone, my sat phone rang. It was the JOC.

"Hey, tell Glen not to shave. We've got a line on 'Z.'"

CHAPTER 14
THE HUNT FOR "Z"

*If you were accused of being a Marine, would
there be enough evidence to convict you?*
—Anonymous

I f you have watched any depiction of special operations troops in
movies, they undoubtedly sported thick, luxurious beards and base-
ball hats. This has become referred to as the special operations "starter
pack." There is often an operational necessity for beards. In many countries where we find ourselves, men are expected to wear beards. It is a
symbol that garners respect.

But for us in 2004, the overarching message was that we needed
to adhere to all Marine Corps standards. There were already plenty of
high-ranking folks within both the Marine Corps and special operations who were looking for reasons to discredit us, and any deviation
from the Marine Corps norm would just add fuel to the fire. We were
told that we would not grow beards without a very significant operational necessity. In protest, most of us chose to grow our best imita-
tions of a 1970s porn star 'stash, which, while still against regulations,
were tolerated.

There are many reasons given for the requirement for Marines
to be clean-shaven. Maintaining short hair and no facial hair lessens
the impact of a lice outbreak when stationed in locations with limited
hygiene resources; long hair gives an enemy something to grab when

battling in hand-to-hand combat; and it can make it impossible to get a gas mask to seal properly. But the biggest reasons are uniformity and discipline. If we all look the same, it is easier to see yourself as a part of the homogenous collective rather than as an individual. Personal style and desires are subjugated for the collective good. It's a bit of a communistic approach, but it works for us. As for discipline, the simple act of doing things that you don't want to do is thought to build it.

The challenge comes because when we select folks for special operations, we look for independent thinkers who can operate in the "gray," a term we use for the ambiguous zone where results can count for more than simple discipline, and where decisive action must often be taken without the benefit of clear orders or directions. The types of people who often thrive in these environments are the same ones who bristle at seemingly mindless orders.

As a young Marine, I was never one to rock the grooming-regulation boat. Life seemed to be much simpler if you kept your hair short and you shaved every day. But when I was in Afghanistan, we were supporting a lieutenant colonel who couldn't wrap his head around the concept of common sense. We were out in the middle of Taliban country in freezing weather, and he insisted that his Marines use their limited water to shave. I refused to have my guys do the same. In addition to the opportunity to be obstinate, my orders made sense. It was foolish to waste not only water but the fuel needed to heat it, when it could be better used to make something hot to drink. There also is always the potential for cuts and infection that follows from quick shaves with cold water. So, I grew my beard and refused to make my guys shave. The lieutenant colonel took to calling me Mullah Dailey.

The Detachment One recon/assault element at our compound, Camp C.W. Myler. (Several faces have been obscured for security.)

Short hair does not build discipline, it simply means that you get frequent haircuts. Don't get me wrong, I am not opposed to maintaining Marine Corps standards, but the fact remains that it is possible to make Grizzly Adams look like a Marine in under thirty minutes with a haircut and shave. When working in an arena where we may need to blend in, the reverse would take a month.

As a redhead, I didn't have much of a dog in the fight. Beard or no, I was never going to pass for an Iraqi; but Glen could, at least at a cursory glance from a distance, or while sitting behind the wheel of a car. And that's the way the planning for Operation Rifle was leaning when we returned from Najaf.

As I've mentioned, we had been targeting "Z" for the entire deployment but still knew very little about him. He led a vast insurgent network that was responsible for scores of assassinations, bombings, and attacks on coalition personnel. "Z" was capable of extreme violence and ruthlessness, but was not reckless. In fact, while many insurgent leaders were targeted because of a slip in their operational security, "Z" remained nearly unassailable. He moved between residences, never staying in the same house for more than a day. His schedule was unpredictable. He kept meetings close-hold and changed locations frequently. All in all, his tradecraft was top-notch. The challenge was finding a gap in the armor.

While we were busy in Najaf, the entire intel section was putting the full-court press on finding that gap. And as usual, when the full weight of the Det intelligence section was directed at a target, it was a nearly unstoppable force.

Eventually, Scotty was able to develop a source with the required placement and access. In our terms, placement and access is defined as an individual's "exploitable proximity to and ability to carry out an intended mission." The initial source operated in the same circles as "Z" but did not have the ability to put him at a particular location at a particular time. For that, they needed to develop a new asset. First, Scotty managed to work another source into the network. This guy represented himself as a well-funded, up-and-coming insurgent from another area of Iraq who was eager to purchase the guns and bombs that his cell needed to destroy Americans. Although his cover held, he was not able to gain access to the inner circle, but during a rare meeting with "Z" he was able to offer a connection. "Z" was looking for an errand boy. Someone to drive him around or pick up things for him. This source indicated that he knew a reliable young man who shared their ideology. Over time, our third source, dubbed "The Kid," was moved into position. "Z" found him reliable because we ensured that he always had a full tank of gas and arrived on time, kept his mouth shut and his ears open. Before long, The Kid was "Z's" primary driver.

One of the most challenging aspects of developing targets within an insurgent network is that the networks are cellular. This limits target vulnerability by reducing the number of cell members known to any one person. On the flip side, it also makes it difficult for an insurgent to verify the bona fides of another insurgent. That's what our guys were banking on when The Kid was introduced to "Z."

I asked Scotty why The Kid would risk so much. It became easy to think that we were fighting for our cause, but there were countless Iraqis who dreamed of better days, who defied death by providing information or support to coalition forces, and who served as interpreters or worked on our bases or joined the new Iraqi military, even though those activities put a price on their heads. But for The Kid it was personal. Scotty told me that his parents had been killed by insurgents. I can't imagine feeling the wrath that he must have felt, yet maintaining his equanimity while driving one of the men who may have been responsible for their deaths.

All of this work had been going on without my knowledge. I simply didn't have the need to know until their efforts began to bear fruit. But while we had been busy in Najaf, Scotty and the other HUMINT guys began closing in on "Z," and now we were brought in to help with the planning.

The Kid notified us about a lunch meeting "Z" was planning. Of course, we preferred nighttime raids and the security that darkness afforded, but you can't always pick the battleground. We gave The Kid a burner phone to communicate with us and a set of coded phrases to transmit, and he worked on confirming the meeting.

The Kid called Scotty and told him that the lunch would happen the following day at a small restaurant in the Mansour district. Although the district encompassed the entire Baghdad Airport complex, the area for the meeting was in an affluent neighborhood on the west side of Baghdad. This wasn't great news. By plotting the location on imagery, we quickly realized how untenable it was. The Kid did not yet have a time, but lunch would obviously be near midday, and the area was packed with shopping and businesses, meaning the streets would be crowded. The location was on a heavily trafficked city street with wide roads, close to several mosques known to be sheltering insurgents. The restaurant's back door opened to a maze of alleyways. Taken together, these facts meant that there was an increased likelihood of collateral damage, and if "Z" made it out of the restaurant he would be swallowed by the throng. And if he slipped through the cracks this time, he would go to ground and we would never get another chance.

Additionally, the crowd could hide fighters. Likely from one of the mosques. We would be hampered in our ability to return fire if the shooting started.

We knew that "Z" was a meticulous planner, so he would have selected the restaurant with escape options at the front of his mind. He would also have observers watching the neighborhood, ready to signal at the first sign of troop movement. We had to expect that our normal exit gates in the BIAP compound were under observation. We decided to prepare and stage within the closest military compound early enough to prevent any connection to the lunch. This would shorten our reaction time, as well as reduce our vulnerability by shortening the route.

There was also simply the matter of scale. Chunks still had some of his team in Najaf wrapping up, so we were shorthanded. To establish a leakproof cordon while limiting our exposure, we would need everybody we could get. We pored over the maps and satellite imagery, discussing options and developing courses of action, or COAs, and wargaming them to find weak spots. The big question was how to get our vehicles close to the target without being spotted. We planned to have a civilian van, driven by Glen in his dishdasha, to get a small force in just a little early.

We worked to get into "Z's" mind. Where would he post observers? How would he communicate? What was his escape plan? Here, the HUMINT Marines were invaluable. They had studied him and were able to provide information on how they believed he had reacted in the past. Generally, the best predictor of future behavior is past behavior. Taking the facts we knew about "Z," we tried to extrapolate how he would react and made educated guesses about *his* most likely and most dangerous courses of action.

There is always a way; it's just usually not the obvious one. Even though we were selected for our ability to think differently and make hard choices, we were also career Marines. We had been trained in the Marine Corps thinking a certain way and solving problems a certain way. The Marine Corps is a hammer-swinging organization, so we often see every problem as a nail.

I can't recall who was gathered around the maps during the planning. The big question on the table was how to cordon off the area quickly without tipping our hand. Although far from verbatim, the conversation went something like this:

"He's gonna have people on these roofs, right?"

"That's what I'd do."

"Well, they'll ID our vehicles as soon as we make the turn here."

"Yeah, if they don't see them sooner."

"He's not going to take a chance. At the first sight of Humvees, he's gone."

As a group, we kicked around ideas and brainstormed. The key to success in this type of planning is to foster divergent thinking and generate lots of ideas, even though many will be impractical, ineffective, or possibly illegal. Once the floodgates of creativity open, it becomes easier to find connections and combine parts of several impractical ideas into one that could work.

"What if we don't use our gun trucks at all? We all go in civilian vehicles."

"Man, we've got to have gun trucks to hold these intersections."

Our normal template for a hard hit meant that we established isolation and containment of the area with gun trucks, hopefully to keep the target in the objective while preparing to address any threats from outside. During midday, those threats were more likely to be awake, alert, and prepared to counterattack.

"Wait, what if the gun trucks roll up after?"

"What do you mean?"

"What if the entire assault force rolls in civilian vans? We keep it small. Go in fast, hit the restaurant, grab "Z," *then* the gun trucks roll up. Maybe we have them staged somewhere."

"We could get the GROM to help."

"Yeah, it could work, unless it doesn't. If the cat gets out of the bag, we're screwed. Those thin-skin vehicles won't provide shit for protection."

"Does anyone see another way?"

A chorus of "Noes" circled the table.

"Then we better keep that cat in the bag."

The other thought that couldn't help but float around in everyone's mind was the possibility that this was a setup. Maybe The Kid had been discovered and turned. Maybe we were heading straight into a complex ambush in the middle of an urban canyon in thin-skinned vans. Images of the Blackwater ambush in Fallujah popped into my head and had to be chased away. It is pointless to focus on the things that you cannot control. That time is far better spent managing the things that you can.

We got the GROM on board, called around to our Green Beret counterparts, and borrowed several panel vans and cargo trucks. For drivers, we identified the guys who could best pass a cursory glance and outfitted them with indigenous garb. The rest of us would be wearing standard kit but would be hidden from view until it was too late to matter.

We moved out early to relocate to our set point, a small base as close as possible to the target restaurant. Then there was nothing to do but wait. Guys slept, read books, did push-ups, or just sat around and talked. The key when waiting like this is to conserve mental energy. You want the amped-up feeling that comes with the unknown. Not too much, but enough to provide the edge that comes with the flow state. I didn't know what it was called then, but I have since read the works of Mihaly Csikszentmihalyi and have a better appreciation of what was going on in our heads then. He described flow as "being completely involved in an activity for its own sake." To maximize performance, the challenge needs to be at the upper end of your capability. Challenging enough to make it interesting, but not too difficult to perform. I felt that each raid we executed met that criterion, or at least offered the potential to meet it, and so we operated in a near-perpetual flow state, where absolutely nothing else exists outside of the present moment and action is autonomic. I had first truly experienced this in Afghanistan, and now got to operate in this state on a near-daily basis. It is addictive. If you got too ramped up too early, the feeling burned out and left you weary. The goal was to meet the challenge with skill. This hit would provide the challenge and would require that level of precision.

"Hey, it's The Kid!" Scotty yelled, grabbing the phone from the hood of the vehicle where he had waited, relentlessly tapping a nervous rhythm on the metal with his thumbs. "Z" had told The Kid to pick him up. We wouldn't depart until we knew "Z" was inside the restaurant, but now was the time to wander over to the row of tan porta-johns that stood next to the sand-filled Hesco barriers that lined the perimeter of the camp. The heat necessitated guzzling liter bottles of water that were recycled several times per day. On our usual nighttime raids, it was pretty easy to find a tree or bush to relieve yourself if needed. There is nothing more uncomfortable than spending hours in full kit and really needing to take a leak. The middle of a busy street at midday wasn't going to make that easy, so we all lined up to go one last time before loading up.

Buzz, Buzz, Buzz. The one-word coded message flashed across the phone's screen. "Let's roll!" Scotty yelled.

I took my place behind Glen, peeking through the curtain we had rigged between the front seats of the panel van. The gates flew open, and he pulled out onto the main road leading downtown. The GROM and their Humvees held back, waiting to give us a head start.

Now we were committed. If we missed "Z," The Kid would certainly be burned. The time, energy, and effort that had gone into establishing his legend and working to get him close to "Z" would be wasted, and the initial source would probably be compromised, as well. Both of their lives, as well as the lives of their families, would be in jeopardy.

I rode on my knees, bracing myself behind Glen's seat and peering out from the corner of the curtain. As we turned off the highway to the route that ran through town, it immediately became congested. Shoppers filled the streets. Cars were bumper-to-bumper, horns honking and cab drivers yelling. Vendors manned stalls on the sidewalk, selling produce and odds and ends. Motor scooters zipped through traffic, sometimes jumping up onto sidewalks to push past jams.

Instead of our usual air support, we relied on calls from an army OH-58D observation helicopter to provide a level of overwatch. The OH-58Ds were such a ubiquitous sight over the area as to not register with the Iraqis.

Murphy's Law states that anything that can go wrong, will. This isn't a sentiment unique to the military, but I have experienced it far more on missions than in civilian life. Because we didn't have the hard-wired antennas that were installed on our Humvees, once we reached the town limits, comm began to falter. The large volume of radio-frequency activity in urban areas can impact communications, but this is why we plan and rehearse contingencies. Everyone knew their roles, so we continued. Then, the navigation system began lagging. Where Ben was usually able to give advance warning of turns based on our position, now the GPS signal was slowed. He called out to Glen, "Let me know what you see, we have to bear left coming up." Behind me, Ben followed the map with his finger, estimating our position and providing directions as best as he could. Fortunately, Glen had memorized the route and was able to stay on course.

I was peeking through the curtain, looking for the right-hand turn where Team Two would split off to secure the back of the building and make entry. With comm down, we needed to rely on everyone knowing their role and executing it flawlessly. I identified the split point and made a radio call I hoped would go through. In the passenger-side mirror, I saw the third truck make the right-hand turn to the alleyway behind the restaurant.

"It's going to be just around the next bend on the right," Ben called out. Everyone raised themselves to a squat, holding on to straps anchored to the sides of the van to keep their balance. As Glen rounded the final curve, I could see the restaurant on our right. A dozen metal tables sprouting large, blue umbrellas that shaded diners covered the wide sidewalk.

Glen called out, "Here we go!" A second later the van jumped the curb. The diners leaped up, believing the vehicle was out of control, but Glen pulled to a quick stop, threw the vehicle into park, and stomped down on the emergency brake. Before I could fully turn, the cargo door was thrown open and shooters were pouring out.

As I jumped from the van, behind us the second van holding Team Six was not fully halted before the side door flew open and Jack's team came barreling for the front door. From the corner of my eye, I caught

Glen coming around the front of the van toward me, then, like Clint Eastwood in *A Fistful of Dollars*, shrugging off the dishdasha, shouldering his rifle, and focusing his attention up the street.

I pushed to my position just outside the front door of the restaurant, trying to calm the diners and keep them from attempting to go inside. Some stood and fled, pulling children behind them by the arms. Others shrugged and went back to their meals. Our job was to secure the exterior, call in the GROM to take up their positions, and deal with any Iraqi military or law enforcement that showed up. Scotty and Captain Thompson moved into the restaurant wearing pictures of "Z" in arm holders similar to those that quarterbacks use to hold plays. The gun truck rounded the corner and took up its blocking position. Any doubt as to what was happening and who was responsible for it was now shattered. If there was going to be an attack, it would happen soon.

There was an impossible amount of area to cover, and far too few of us. My eyes darted from the shadows of doorways to rooftops to the hands of passersby who were now giving us a wide berth. Scanning hands and eyes for triggers and intent. Each passing car was a potential Vehicle Borne Improvised Explosive Device (VBIED), each shopper a body bomb.

Scotty obviously recognized The Kid, but had to play it cool. He sat at a round table near the back of the restaurant with a group of men. One with his back to the wall matched the photo. In front of them sat steaming cups of tea, barely tasted. Team Two shooters burst through the kitchen door, and there were a dozen rifle barrels pointed at the men around the table. "Z" calmly placed his hands on the table, the others followed his lead, and they were taken without a fight. The Kid was cuffed and blindfolded with the rest of them. He would need to be held, to maintain his cover and ensure his safety. The back door offered the least exposure, so the detainees were moved through the kitchen to the waiting vehicles. Once they were loaded, a codeword was passed over the radio and we mounted back up and left the GROM to bring up the rear.

It was only after getting "Z" to the detention facility, and the word got around that we had captured him, that I began to understand how important a figure he was. We were congratulated and thanked for the work, but told that he would be taken off of our hands and that his interrogation would be handled by a higher authority. Nonetheless, this one felt good.

Based in part on our successes, we were handed another target. This one, Objective Ruby, was a former regime element (FRE) general and a cousin of Saddam. He held a place on the famous Iraqi Most Wanted deck of cards. He had been responsible, in part, for the atrocities visited upon the Shi'ites and Kurds in 1991. After the short-lived Gulf War, Saddam was seen as vulnerable, and a loosely formed alliance launched a series of uprisings between March and April 1991. The uprising stalled after a promising beginning, due to a lack of coordination and when the hoped-for US support didn't materialize. Once Saddam's Ba'athist regime regained the initiative, they struck back with a vengeance, allegedly using chemical weapons in attacks to retake the city of Basra, and toxic chemicals were dumped in waterways to drive out the Marsh Arabs. All told, tens of thousands of Iraqis were killed in the reprisals, and hundreds of thousands of refugees fled, seeking sanctuary in Iran and Turkey. So yeah, we wanted him.

We planned the mission targeting a residence that he had reportedly been seen at. We ran rehearsals and went through our normal preparation. The hit was scheduled to take place the following night.

I was glad to be back to conducting nighttime raids. We pulled out of Camp Myler after midnight, quickly getting back into the usual rhythm. The vehicles dropped us off a block from the house and we moved quickly but silently, setting ladders and scaling the wall. I pulled security while the breach team worked. After the thump of the explosion, I turned and moved into the house, taking the stairway to the upper floor. Mike, Ben, Eric, and I rotated though the rooms, clearing each, then picking up on the next doorway.

We had nearly reached the end of the hall when a shout carried through the house: *"Red Rocket!"*

It was the call that an IED had been found. The call was echoed by everyone who heard it: *"Red Rocket!" "Red Rocket!" "Red Rocket!"* It was passed verbally, because there was concern that our radio signals might set off the device. We began to pull back, maintaining security while the EOD techs rolled in to look. As soon as they observed the device, they passed the code word "Landslide," the call to evacuate the building, which was more reassuring than the codeword "Avalanche," which meant "jump out of the nearest window and run."

Outside, Major Kozeniesky was trying to get enough information to make a decision: disarm the device or leave? He called for sitreps from the team leaders. I passed "Didn't see or hear anything upstairs, two rooms left uncleared."

Before a decision was reached, the device began beeping and the EOD techs explosively disabled it.

The building was a "dry hole." We moved to an adjacent structure and detained the occupants, who told us that the target lived in the house, but they claimed that they had not seen him for some time. Scotty was working through the interpreter to gather as much information from the neighbors as possible when an explosion near one of our containment teams rocked the night. From another direction came bursts of gunfire directed at another position. Col K radioed us all to load back up, and we headed back to Camp Myler.

We didn't know it then, but Objective Ruby was the last raid of our deployment. We knew our time was nearly up, but hoped for one more opportunity. We wanted to finish on a high note. Meanwhile, we began packing up, making initial preparations to return. A few days later, I was called into the JOC. Captain Thompson sat behind a computer with a map pulled up on the screen.

"Ranger, the army is having trouble with a sniper in Hawija. Interested?"

CHAPTER 15

SPAM AND SNIPERS

War is hell, but that's not the half of it, because
war is also mystery and terror and adventure
and courage and discovery and holiness and
pity and despair and longing and love.
—Tim O'Brien

There wasn't much information available on the Hawija sniper. We would have to wait until we linked up with the army unit in the area to get filled in. We would be working with the First Battalion, Twenty-Seventh Infantry Regiment, Twenty-Fifth Infantry Division, known as "The Wolfhounds." They were a part of the famed "Tropic Lightning" Division based out of Schofield Barracks, Hawaii. One of the unit's more literary former members, James Jones, wrote *From Here to Eternity*, based on his experiences in the Twenty-Seventh.

Because the sniper had been taking a toll, 1/27 had reached out to the local Special Forces ODA in the area. They were unable to support, so the call was put out through SOCOM channels, and we were happy to make the trip.

We didn't know what the future held for us back at Camp Myler, so to keep as much of our combat power available for HVT targeting, I was only able to bring one other guy. I didn't hesitate for a second in picking Mike. We worked well together, and he was an incredibly competent sniper. With his calm demeanor, he also had the ability to temper my tendency to rush into things. He would usually preface his suggestions with: "Yeah, well, we could do that, but don't you think…?" I had learned to listen when he offered input.

This is one of the strengths of special-operations organizations. In traditional military units, it is often the officer in charge who thinks the big thoughts and makes the tactical decisions and translates them to the enlisted personnel on the team. One of the great things about reconnaissance units is that teams are led by enlisted men, and while the rank structure still exists and is important, it was rarely a consideration. As a leader, it was seldom necessary to remind anyone that you were the leader. In a highly motivated and superbly trained small team, everyone has equal skin in the game, and everyone brings something a little different to the table. I have found that the biggest challenge as a leader is to determine how to best leverage each person's strengths against the mission. And, for a sniper mission, Mike was the guy I wanted with me.

We packed up enough equipment and ammunition to last a few days. Knowing that the Wolfhounds would be able to take care of our food and lodging, we went heavy on ammo. While we packed, the intel guys printed maps covering the Hawija area and provided us with a quick synopsis of what we were likely heading into.

Hawija is a town roughly 190 miles north of Baghdad, in Kirkuk Province. Primarily populated by Sunnis, a significant Sunni insurgency was active in and around the town and was responsible for numerous attacks against coalition forces. It was considered at the time to be one of the most dangerous locations in Iraq and earned the nickname "Anbar of the North," as a reference to the incredibly violent Al Anbar Province in western Iraq.

Mike and I caught a ride out to the LZ where a waiting Blackhawk flew us to the airfield in Kirkuk. There we spent the night before traveling to Hawija. The airfield was massive, with dirt-filled Hesco barriers, concertina wire, and monolithic concrete slabs providing concentric rings of security. We were met by a SOCOM liaison and handed off to an air force sergeant. He helped us load our rucks and rifles into a pickup and began the process of weaving us through the multiple layers of security, finally arriving at a small, maze-like trailer park reserved for visitors.

Although the trailers were closely spaced, each was separated from the next by concrete barriers meant to limit the damage of a mortar or rocket attack, but which served to provide a feeling of complete isolation. We seemed to be the only visitors, but it was hard to say. Once we each claimed a rack and made sure that all our equipment was prepped, we dragged two plastic lawn chairs out into the gravel courtyard. To catch a view of the night sky beyond the trailer walls and concrete, it was necessary to lean way back and look almost straight up. We had been so used to working the night shift that neither of us could sleep, even though we knew we would a long day ahead of us. The curse of the third-shift worker.

Neither of us smoked, but Mike pulled out some Cuban cigars, which could be purchased legally in Iraq, and we puffed away. He mentioned having brought a tub of Tang that he had received in a care package. I produced a flask of vodka, and we invented a cocktail dubbed "The Cosmonaut," which is prepared by adding two scoops of Tang and several jiggers of vodka to eight ounces of desert-temperature bottled water. The cocktail is then shaken and served in the same plastic water bottle. I have since recreated the drink on several occasions with ice and an appropriate highball glass, but I can't recreate the magic.

The stillness of the night was disturbed by the occasional helo lifting off or landing, the heat made only slightly more bearable because the sun was down. The grit of the desert worked its way into every sip of the sugary drink. Still, we sat outside enjoying the brilliance of the stars and talking about home and our families until the vodka was depleted. We had both served at First Force Recon for several years before we met. That wasn't an uncommon occurrence for those in different platoons. If the unit was insular, each platoon was a world unto itself. Deployments and training cycles meant that we often never connected. It was Tracy who met Mike's wife, Amy, and introduced us. We discovered that we lived just several houses apart and our children played in the backyard playground. Our sons shared the name Garrett.

I recently had the chance to catch up with Mike. His children, like mine, are grown and his nest is nearly empty. He is certain that it was a flask of Jim Beam rather than vodka, which certainly seems possible, but I can't remember it that way. It also makes the name "Cosmonaut" far less on the nose.

The next morning, we were met by members of the Special Forces Operational Detachment Alpha (ODA). They were to transport us to their home at Forward Operating Base (FOB) Gaines Mills, which was halfway between Kirkuk and Hawija. The FOB sat atop a piece of high ground surrounded by open desert and fields. "Wolfhound" soldiers manned the gate and checkpoints along the perimeter. The ODA was housed in a series of small, earth-colored buildings set away from the remainder of the FOB. When we arrived, several members of the ODA were practicing hand-to-hand combat under a camouflage net for shade.

We were led into a lounge area where we sat on couches and were soon joined by the ODA team leader and team sergeant. They explained that the ODA was task-saturated and appreciated the support. The team shared what they knew about the sniper and the area. The team sergeant coordinated a ride for us to the base at Hawija. We shook hands and exchanged frequencies and call signs, then loaded up for the hazardous drive out to the Wolfhound headquarters in Hawija.

Before he shut the armored door he leaned in. "Hey, y'all call us if you get into trouble or need anything."

"Will do. Thanks."

Once we were dropped off, we found our way into the combat operations center and introduced ourselves to the operations officer (OPSO). He sent a runner to grab the unit's snipers and led us to meet the unit commander, who thanked us for making the trip and promised his full support. The OPSO then led us into the section of the building that housed the intelligence section. We were shaking hands with the intel officer when two sweaty soldiers burst in.

The trio led us to the far side of the building, to a room with an old wooden-framed corkboard holding a map and pieces of overhead imagery. Colored pushpins indicated locations where soldiers had been shot, and others estimated the sniper's firing position. Around the periphery, black-and-white photos of the suspected shooting positions were pinned.

We later learned that the unit's "snipers" were part of the unit's marksmanship-training section. While they were good men and undoubtedly brave soldiers, they had not been trained as snipers. And while they were doing their best to provide the commander with information, they were making some assumptions that would prove unlikely.

Before they directed our attention to the map, the lead sniper filled us in on the enemy shooter that had been dubbed "the dentist of Hawija." As the name implied, according to the legend, our shooter had once been a dentist in the town with a wife and several children. The stories varied depending on who was telling them, but the gist was that his wife and children had been killed by American munitions, and he swore revenge. In most versions of the story, "The Dentist" was able to get his hands on an old Russian SVD sniper rifle and a seemingly unlimited supply of ammunition. He wandered into the desert where he taught himself to shoot and emerged highly skilled and bent on destroying Americans.

It is axiomatic that the biggest enemy is your own mind. When you imbue an enemy with near-supernatural powers, you will begin to see him that way and interpret any available information in a way that confirms your opinion. This is confirmation bias. Once this image has taken hold it spreads, and it is difficult to change opinions.

According to their "forensics," the enemy sniper was taking one-thousand-yard-plus headshots. The primary target had been gunners standing in the turrets of Humvees manning their machine guns. Usually, the vehicle was moving, often quite quickly. When they began to point out the suspected firing positions, I looked at Mike, and he looked at me. We followed the bullet path traced on the map by a finger.

"What makes you think the shots were taken from so far away?"

"We started our search close, then expanded out. This spot offers the best concealment. And no one heard the shot."

"Could he have a suppressor?" I asked. At this point in the war, we hadn't run into enemy forces using suppressors. It wasn't likely that a self-trained sniper would have one.

"They were in moving vehicles. It's not a surprise they didn't hear anything," Mike offered.

I shook my head. "Yeah, I think we need to look closer. That's a long shot."

"Man, this guy is good," one of the men offered.

"So am I, but I wouldn't risk that shot," I said. "It's a low-percentage shot. I'd get closer."

Mike pointed to the aerial imagery, "Aren't these buildings, between the firing position and the target, in the way?"

"We checked it out. He's shooting through multiple loopholes."

A loophole, in sniper parlance, is a small opening that allows the shooter to remain hidden from view while firing, like the drain hole in the parapet of a rooftop in Najaf. If you can place additional loopholes between yourself and the target, you will absolutely make it more difficult to find your location. The problem is that this is much easier said than done.

Once a round leaves the barrel of a rifle, it is influenced by two factors: velocity and gravity. The mass of the projectile determines how strongly gravity will pull, and as soon as it leaves the barrel, velocity begins to fall off, and with it, kinetic energy.

When shooting a typical .30 caliber bullet at one thousand yards, the flight path is a parabola, with the maximum height at the midrange being somewhere around thirty feet above the straight line from the shooter to the target. This point is the "maximum ordinate." To shoot through multiple loopholes, imagine a path out of a window in one building, through windows on either side of an intermediate building, to the target. To make that shot you would need to be able to accurately determine the trajectory of the round along its full path. And at a thousand yards, the windows of the intermediate building would be three stories above your head. This also means that you would need to account for the wind at the maximum ordinate, which, especially in an urban environment, could be significantly different from that in the shooter's position, and which will have the greatest effect on the path of the bullet. I don't like to say that something is impossible, but I do usually subscribe to Occam's Razor, which tells us that the simplest explanation is usually the best.

But it wasn't going to be helpful to explain the intricacies of ballistics at that particular moment. I said something along the lines of, "Alright, I think we have a decent idea of what you guys are up against. Can you guys show us where we're staying, and then we can start brainstorming options."

"Sure, we've got you bunking with us, if that's OK."

"Sounds good to me. Let's go."

They led Mike and me to a lone, plywood B-Hut set away from the others.

"We've got a couple of extra cots. It ain't much, but it's home."

One of the soldiers we hadn't met yet chimed in, "For one more month, anyway."

"Oh, shit. You guys are short-timers, huh?" I asked.

"Yeah. That's what's frustrating. The CO isn't interested in going after The Dentist. He doesn't want to lose anybody else, but we want to nail that fucker before we leave."

Mike and I picked empty cots and lay our rifles down, then dropped our rucks to the floor.

"You guys hungry?"

I looked at my watch. It was around 2:00 p.m. "I could eat. Are they serving chow now?

"No. But we are going to cook some Spam."

"Oh, OK, sure."

We turned back around to the doorway, and I saw what I had missed before. The entryway walls were lined with cans of Spam. There must have been at least a hundred cans stacked like bricks against the wall.

I did not know it at the time, but Spam is huge in Hawaii. It was introduced to the island during WWII and was a big hit. Although none of these guys were Hawaiian by birth, they had latched onto Spam in a big way. So, we went outside and sat around the fire pit.

Soon a skillet was smoking, and slabs of Spam were tossed in to fry. Once done, the skillet was passed around, with each man stabbing a slice with his pocketknife. During the time we were there, this scene was repeated eight to ten times each day. I don't think I saw them eat anything else.

As we had our fill of Spam, the senior guy told us that they had been pushing the commander to let them tackle the sniper problem, but he was reluctant. They thought that having some SOF snipers help out would get him to take action. They let us know that the unit had cut back to minimal patrols, limiting any movement outside of the wire as much as possible.

Mike and I were sure that the enemy shooter didn't possess the skills they were attributing to him, and felt that if we could draw him out, we stood a good chance of taking him down.

At the time, I felt that the commander was a coward, unwilling to take the measures necessary to provide the chance of killing the sniper responsible for the casualties among his troops. Now I have a better appreciation for his predicament. I was fortunate to never lose a man under my charge in combat, so I can only imagine the difficulty of each decision he made, the sleepless hours spent replaying events and wondering what he could have done differently, the anguish over each line of letters penned to the wives and mothers of the fallen.

But we had been sent there to take care of the sniper, so at the time, that is what I was focused on. Mike and I worked to convince our compatriots that we needed to dial back the perceived invincibility of this shooter and focus on the things we knew. We developed several plans to hopefully entice the shooter to show himself. We helped our Spam-eating buddies build dummy torsos to extend from gun turrets. We requested permission to head out on our own and take up positions to observe the limited vehicle patrols that were taking place. We selected a high point that provided good coverage of the area we suspected the shooter was using. The commander denied our request.

We tagged along on the patrols that did go out. On one, a cautious driver identified an IED in a pile of rubbish on the side of the road. A radio call went out. The vehicles in the kill-zone sped past. All others reversed out of the area to take up defensive positions. Mike and I sat sweltering in the back of an armored gun truck waiting for the order to disembark. There we were sitting ducks for rockets.

"We need to un-ass this vehicle and pick up security," I said.

"Negative, we're holding tight. It might be a trap."

"Exactly. We need to move, Mike. Come on."

Against the protests, we jumped out of the vehicle and ran to a partially demolished, multistory building. We took the stairs up to the second floor and then set up our rifles to provide overwatch. Several blocks away an explosion rocked us. It seems that it was a prematurely detonated IED, and no one was injured. We scanned the windows and rooftops, looking for movement or a glint of glass, but saw nothing. Eventually, the EOD squad arrived to disarm the IED, and we loaded up and returned to base.

As much as we wanted to help, it was pointless to remain if we weren't going to be allowed to do anything to help. I went into the unit's operations center to let the OPSO know. I told him that I didn't feel like we were helping, and that we needed to get back to Camp Mylar. He understood my frustration but told me about a meeting that would be taking place the following afternoon. This was an obligation that needed to be kept: a meeting with the commander and the local government representatives.

"If I wanted to shoot some Americans, that's where I would be," the OPSO said.

"Can we get in on it?"

"Yeah, if you're sticking around."

"Another day won't hurt. Can you show me where on the map?"

He pointed to a location in the heart of the city, then explained how the meeting would go, where the vehicles would drop the commander off, where he would walk to enter the building for the meeting, and where the vehicles would take up security positions.

A block away, a tall building stood several floors above the rest.

"What's this building?" I asked, pointing to the imagery.

"I don't know what it is, but you can access it."

"This will give us the best vantage point. If I was The Dentist, I would consider using it. We'll need to clear it. Can we get a few guys to help us? Then we'll set up here on the top floor. We will be able to cover the meeting and hopefully pick him up if he shows."

"I'll run it by the commander, but I think it makes sense."

The next afternoon the lead vehicle dropped us off on the way to the meeting. We didn't have any time to spare, so we quickly pushed into the building, rapidly clearing the rooms with windows overlooking the meeting place, heading for the top floor. Our sniper rifles were slung, and we cleared with pistols out. When we reached the top floor, Mike put his hand on the doorknob and looked at me. I nodded and he threw the door open.

We entered to find a small room that had been used for storage. We moved to the window, opened it, and stacked up some old trunks to make a quick shooting position. The lead vehicle was just rounding the corner and pulling to a stop in front of the meeting place. We scanned rooftops and windows, looking for anything abnormal—a shadow, a glare—but nothing seemed out of the ordinary. The commander and his entourage entered the building, and the soldiers took positions of cover.

As we sat scanning, Mike reached across and grabbed my arm. When I looked at him, he pointed to the door. Then I heard it—a creak on the steps, then a knock at the door. We threw the door open to find an old lady who had probably had plenty of weapons pointed at her in her time. She barely flinched, then stepped inside with a tray holding a pot of steaming tea and several small teacups. She looked around for a place to set the tray, poured two cups full, and walked out.

"Shukran," I called after her. *Thanks*.

The meeting concluded sometime later without incident. Mike and I pooled our resources to leave a few dinars on the tray.

The next morning, we packed up, thanked our hosts, and after a hearty breakfast of Spam, caught a ride to Kirkuk, then finagled a Blackhawk back to Camp Mylar.

CHAPTER 16
THE BEGINNING OF THE END

*But a sense of strangeness will not leave me. I cannot
feel at home among these things. There is my mother,
there is my sister, there is my case of butterflies, and
there is the mahogany piano, but I am not myself
there. There is a distance, a veil between us.*
—Erich Maria Remarque

Our return from Hawija signaled the beginning of the end. The guys who had been farmed out to work with SEAL teams or other agencies returned. We greeted them and exchanged stories. We hoped for a final mission, but there was nothing actionable that we could turn around quickly. Just as we arrived without a unit to turn over with, we would be leaving Camp Myler without anyone to replace us. Our working-target folders were divvied up and passed out to the Special Forces ODAs around Baghdad.

We spent our final days in-country cleaning gear and reviewing and documenting the things we had learned. Our whole existence as a unit had been a proof of concept, so analysts arrived to ask questions and take notes, to try to quantify the impact we had and turn it into written reports and PowerPoint pie charts. Then even they were gone, and all that was left was to pack up what we had brought, load it into rucks and bags and shipping containers, and load them onto trucks to be further loaded onto aircraft for the trip home.

I find leaving always bittersweet. Yes, I was eager to get home and see Tracy and the kids, but I couldn't help but wonder if we did enough. We felt we had made a difference and had taken some key players off the board, but fighting an insurgency is a game of whack-a-mole. Soon after you smash one in the head, another pops up somewhere else. All you can do is keep smashing until your arms are tired, and another player steps in to grab the mallet.

A unit never leaves anywhere all at once. There is always an advance party to prepare for the main unit's arrival, and a rear party left to pick up any pieces and make sure that we didn't forget anything important. But on the night of September 27, the bulk of the Det loaded vehicles for one final night drive. At Baghdad International, we lugged and loaded gear, then buckled in for the short field take-off. The C-17 jerked into the sky by brute force, gaining elevation as rapidly as 250 tons can, to thwart missiles. Then the pitch of the engines changed, the aircraft leveled out, and we were off, Iraq behind us. A few men cheered or slapped each other on the back. We had done well. Really well. And we all wondered what would come next.

After a twenty-four-hour layover in Ankara, Turkey, spent doing our best to drink the country dry, we slept through the next leg of the trip, awakened for a brief stop to refuel in Nova Scotia before finally landing at the Marine Corps Air Station in Miramar, California. There we went through customs inspection and loaded buses. At that time of evening, it was just a quick forty-five-minute drive back to Camp Delmar.

It was early morning when we returned to the compound. Still dark out. The families were gathered to greet us. Mothers held sleepy children, some wearing pajamas while others ran around the compound. I picked Tracy, Garrett, and Kallie out of the crowd and went to them. Returning from deployment is like seeing your children grow in snapshots taken a half year apart. As we stood hugging and catching up, we watched Mike's son, Garrett, now probably six years old, run up to the first set of camouflage legs he saw and hug them—then run away crying when he realized the legs didn't belong to his dad. I suspect that this scene is played every time a unit returns. Children looking to reconnect with a parent that they know best only through stories and photos, or videos of beach days and Christmas mornings.

My words for these reunions are inadequate. Seeing Tracy, Garrett, and Kallie after such a long separation is overwhelming. Seeing how the kids had grown and changed is scary. They like different TV shows, music, have different friends, different hobbies than they did just a half year ago. When I feel regret at missing milestones, I have to remind myself that I chose this life, and knowing what that meant, Tracy chose me. The kids had no say in the matter; but kids are resilient, and they always handled it like champs.

Tracy swallows a mixture of resentment and anger when civilian friends complain that their spouse has to go away for a week on business, or when the wives of military husbands who somehow seemed to avoid leaving home whine when they were finally compelled to deploy in relative safety. I wouldn't say that I begrudge them. I wanted to be where the action was, with others who wanted the same. I thrived on it, and so I reserved my regret for the contemplative period that followed each homecoming. And truly, it didn't last long before I was itching to start preparing to go again. It was just something in my nature, I guess.

While I had been gone, Tracy had been saving money and planning a real family vacation. A trip to Hawaii. After a week or two of taking care of business around the compound, we got the opportunity to take a long block of leave. We flew out of Los Angeles and spent a week together as a family, snorkeling and sightseeing, taking early-morning walks, late-evening luaus, and tasting poi. I felt no urge to hunt down any Spam.

I had hoped that by the time I returned to work, we would have an idea of what was next. We all felt confident that we had proven the concept of Marine SOF, and we would redeploy; we just needed to know when and where. But when we returned from leave, Colonel Coates didn't have any new answers, so we were left to rumor and speculation. The consensus of our speculation was that we would be sent to Afghanistan to operate in a different environment and prove ourselves there. The idea made enough sense that, as we returned to training, we focused on that possibility.

While we were training, Colonel Coates and the staff were busy fighting for our existence. They attended countless after-action debriefs and high-level meetings with the USMC and SOCOM leadership. Obviously, I was not invited to any of these meetings, so my comments are part hearsay and part speculation. From our perspective, we felt the eventual decision by SOCOM and the Marine Corps was a reflection of their opinion of our success in combat. We knew we had kicked ass and that we deserved to stay and grow. It was impossible to understand why these discussions were even happening. We had proven our value, and it seemed that a positive decision should have been fait accompli.

The smart money was on the idea that we would soon be able to begin recruitment to build a Detachment Two. We gathered to discuss the best way to accomplish this. It seemed that splitting each team, then filling in with replacements, was the best bet—like a cell reproducing. We came up with a plan for who would remain in Det-One and who would shift to Det-Two. A small group was tasked with developing a multiday assessment-and-selection program that could be executed at Camp Pendleton.

We had been known quantities, handpicked, but that came at a cost to Force Recon and intelligence units across the Marine Corps. If we were going to grow, we needed to expand our aperture and allow more Marines to try out. Almost all the Det-One Recon Marines had come from First Force Recon at Camp Pendleton. We would need to open the opportunity to the recon units in Camp Lejeune, North Carolina and Okinawa, Japan.

An unwritten rule in the Marines is that you never ask someone to do something that you haven't yourself done. So once the plan for our assessment-and-selection program was finalized, we decided to test it out. Half of us would participate, the other half would provide the necessary safety and support, and then we would switch.

I'm not sure how we decided, but I of course wound up in the participating half. Because we were only going to be drawing our replacements from the reconnaissance community, we knew that we could make some assumptions about physical conditioning; but we wanted to see what would happen when we pushed people to their breaking point. Could they still make good decisions? Could they keep their cool under pressure? And could they keep going alone, without a team around them to rely on?

The first day of assessment measured overall fitness, agility, strength, and shooting skills. Day two included road marches and obstacle courses, more shooting, and swimming. Then that evening, after a full day of activity, we launched into an individual land-navigation exercise that covered nearly fifty miles through the steep hills and canyons of Camp Pendleton's training areas. We were looking for men with strong backs and hard feet, men who could—to quote Rudyard Kipling—"force your heart and nerve and sinew to serve your turn long after they are gone, and so hold on when there is nothing in you except the will which says to them: 'Hold on!'"

It was late in the afternoon the following day when I hit my last navigation point. I think it was Ben who was manning the point. He said something to the effect of, "OK, that's it. Good work. Now you just need to get home."

Of course, "home" was nearly twenty miles away.

"Great. Swell. Thanks." I turned, oriented myself, and took off at a jog. "I'll see you back there, bastard!"

He called from behind me, "Everybody wants to be Recon until it's time to do recon shit."

I seem to recall flipping him off, but after thirty-six hours of continual movement, memories are hard to pin down.

Throughout the discussion of our future, one thing we knew was that Commander Bill Wilson was in our corner. I know he faced some institutional resistance for endorsing us. Not everyone in the SEAL community was excited about a new SOF unit competing for missions—although according to the official Marine Corps historical division report on Det-One, written by Lieutenant Colonel John Piedmont, the commander of Naval Special Warfare, Rear Admiral Joseph McGuire, was "openly laudatory."

In December 2004, Colonel Coates and (now) Lieutenant Colonel Kozeniesky presented an After-Action Review to the Commandant of the Marine Corps, General Michael Hagee, and the SOCOM commander, General Bryan Brown. By the end of the meeting, it was clear that neither general believed that there was a future for the detachment beyond the end of our two-year charter, which was set to end on February 20, 2005. The two generals owed a recommendation to Secretary of Defense Donald Rumsfeld in January. And so, while held in purgatory, we did what we could: train.

Glen and I made a trip out to Texas to visit Todd Hodnett. He had continued to immerse himself in the world of training long-range shooters. Todd welcomed us into his home, and we enjoyed a week with him and his family. Our days were spent on the open plains of their West Texas ranch, shooting at distances of a mile or more, testing out several .338 rifles and scope combinations. The .338 is a much bigger and faster cartridge than our standard .308, and it excels at long distance. But at a mile, the round was hitting its highest point along its trajectory (maximum ordinate) at nearly 150 feet above the straight line to the target. Winds that high above the shooter can be unpredictable and will play havoc with horizontal impacts. At these distances, you also have to calculate for gyroscopic spin drift and the Coriolis effect. As implausible as it may seem, at extreme ranges the rotation of the earth affects the strike of a rifle shot; so, in addition to gravity, drag, humidity, wind, and other environmental factors, we now had to concern ourselves with the spin of the earth. When shooting to the east, the target is getting closer and the bullet will strike high, to the west farther away. To add to the confusion, shooting north and south depends on not only the direction you are shooting, but how close to the equator you are. For a guy who barely squeaked through Algebra 1, the fact that I learned to make the litany of necessary calculations is a huge testament to Todd's knowledge and patience.

Each evening we returned to Todd's house to clean rifles and enjoy his family's Texas hospitality. Then, once darkness fell, we checked the batteries in our night-vision scopes and headed out to help eradicate the feral boar that plagued the ranch. Stalking and shooting the animals at night proved immensely challenging and was fantastic training, and the meat wasn't too bad.

While we trained with Todd, we made plans for him to conduct a training course for our snipers. We selected a location in southern Utah that would provide challenging wind and terrain for shooting at long ranges and at high angles.

After each training opportunity, we returned to the compound hoping for some new information, and dreading that when it came it would be unfavorable. The commandant and SOCOM commander notified Secretary Rumsfeld that they "did not see a clear requirement for Det-One to continue." Meanwhile, our scheduled February 20 deactivation date passed without comment, which we took as a good omen. While most of us were held in limbo, inevitably some Marines moved on to other jobs. Recently promoted to Lieutenant Colonel, Kozeniesky was reassigned and replaced as operations officer by Lieutenant Colonel Frank Donovan, who had a long recon and special-operations pedigree. We saw that as another positive sign.

Lieutenant Colonel Donovan brought with him an idea for a concept of employment that we felt would serve us well. One of the challenges US forces faced in targeting remote camps in the Afghanistan mountains was that a team couldn't remain concealed for too long. They could predictably insert into an area by helicopter, with a long offset and movement by foot or ATVs to get eyes on a target, but it was rare for a team to last for more than twenty-four hours without becoming compromised. Little happens in the desert that goes unobserved by those who know what they are looking for. The best-case scenario in a compromise is that the news of our proximity gets to the intended target who then flees; the worst is that the team gets caught in a gunfight with a numerically superior force, without the ability to reinforce.

While we were searching for a way to attack the problem, in June 2005 this scenario played out with deadly consequences on an Afghanistan mountainside. SEALs Michael Murphy, Danny Dietz, Matthew Axelson, and Marcus Luttrell were inserted into the Hindu Kush to locate terrorist leader Ahmad Shah. Early in the mission, dubbed Operation Red Wings, they were compromised by locals who reported their location to the terrorists. Only Luttrell would survive the ensuing gunfight. This brought back the ethical dilemma of the shepherd, posed to me so many years ago during the Force Recon Indoc: "What do you do, Dailey?"

The standard template had been to insert reconnaissance-and-surveillance teams to pinpoint the target, and once confirmed, bring in an assault force to attack. What if, we wondered, one team could do both? A team large enough and moving light enough, but with all the required equipment to pinpoint the target, and then assault while we still held the advantage to surprise?

The best place to begin developing the tactics required for this sort of mission was the Mountain Warfare Training Center at Bridgeport, California, so we returned several times, operating as an opposing force to infantry units conducting their regular training. We experimented with loads, shaving ounces to make pounds, moving with minimal food, water, and cold-weather gear, trying to get as light as possible. We sought inspiration from the lightweight-backpacking movement and books like Ray Jardine's *Beyond Backpacking*, striking a balance between necessity and survivability. At times we were forced to forego the age-old mantra of "two is one, and one is none," and fully embrace the other mantra: "travel light, freeze at night."

We had shifted teams. Now I got to work with different guys, Andy and Big H. But we all woke each day wondering if the rumor would change, or if some decision would be made; and each morning when we were back at the compound, we would gather for the morning formation hoping for some solid word about our future.

What we couldn't know was that although the two generals had recommended ending the experiment and not continuing a Marine Corps contribution to USSOCOM, Secretary Rumsfeld was not buying it. He directed them to go back to the drawing board and provide a plan to create the United States Marines Corps Special Operations Command.

In July, Glen and I met up with Todd at the piece of private property we were using for training. The land was once mined for uranium. Now neglected mine entrances yawned in the hillsides. The property's owner showed us around with a Geiger counter strapped around his neck, to show us the caves were safe to occupy. We set up cots inside to get out of the high desert heat.

To maximize the training opportunity, we split the Det snipers into two groups. The first arrived for a two-week training package, then we swapped out. Glen and I stayed with Todd for the month. While I can't say that I love the desert, there is something about it. Especially in the early mornings before the sun rises, when the sky and sand begin to turn pink. I loved to wake up early to go for a long run, exploring canyons and scrambling up hillsides, returning to grab a cup of coffee and sit alone to drink it as our camp slowly came to life. Each morning we went out for a session of shooting, returning for lunch to the coolness of the caves for a long siesta. We contracted the local sheriff/chef to cook dinner for us, which usually consisted of Navajo tacos or chili-covered pasta cooked over a campfire. After gorging ourselves, we headed back out for night shooting.

It is challenging to find locations to practice shooting at extreme angles. So, while we had all been taught the fundamentals, getting to practice under multiple scenarios was enlightening. Angle-shooting, of course, requires a whole additional set of mathematical principles, calculations, and cosigns to determine the correct ballistic data to use to make the shot.

It was a great month with no television and no cell service. Todd and I swapped books and had long discussions around the campfire. He was reading about kyudo, the art of Japanese Zen archery. It was easy to see the similarities between that discipline and sniping. We tried to embrace the philosophy of the discipline captured in its motto, *Issha Zetsumei*, translated as "One shot and expire." From that, I took the idea of putting everything into each shot so that you would be satisfied if it were your last act, and marveled at how similar the philosophy was to the Stoics. It reminded me of the quote by Marcus Aurelius: "You could leave life right now. Let that determine what you do and say and think."

After we returned from the desert, a group of us went back to Utah, this time to Salt Lake City to spend a month training with ODAs from the Second Battalion, Fifth Special Forces Group, focusing on surveillance, surveillance detection, urban operations, and working with their human-intelligence specialists.

As we prepared to return to combat, in Washington and Quantico, Virginia, decisions were being made. The United States Marine Corps Special Operations Command was going to be a reality. MARSOC, for short, would evolve into an organization of several thousand Marines and sailors led by a two-star general. While we were proud to see this, we also felt that Colonel Coates should have had more involvement in the decision-making process. Det-One would not factor into the plans for the new organization. Like the kyudo motto: One shot and expire.

Those of us who remained had to seek out our own leadership positions in the new command, which would be headquartered at Camp Lejeune, North Carolina. Mike and I asked to be sent to the command's new school. If my experience at SOTG had taught me anything, it was that change begins at the bottom. If you want to impact the way an organization operates, change the entry-level training. Tracy and Mike's wife, Amy, flew out to North Carolina to look for homes. Tracy returned with photos of a still-under-construction house just a few miles outside of the base, in a new neighborhood filled with other Marines and children.

The last months were a whirlwind of preparing to move while preparing to close the shutters on the Det. Our belongings were packed up, and we moved from base housing to a cottage on the beach for the final few days, living out of suitcases.

On the afternoon of March 10, 2006, on the same patch of asphalt where the experiment began, it ended. This time between spring showers. Families and guests, retired generals, and WWII Raiders sat on wet metal bleachers with umbrellas at the ready. We stood together in formation one last time, heedless of the "recon sunshine" falling from the sky. Someone read a commendation from the Secretary of the Navy which said, in part:

> Taking full advantage of their advanced skills, unique training, and specialized equipment, the Marines and Sailors of Marine Corps Special Operations Command Detachment One aggressively sought opportunities to locate and destroy an elusive enemy, inflicting

significant damage on the Iraq insurgent movement, resulting in the safe and expeditious transfer of authority to the Interim Iraqi Government and safety of principal government officials. Detachment One's accomplishments proved conclusively that the Marine Corps could operate at the level of other special operations units and contributed directly to the Secretary of Defense's decision to add a US Marine Corps component to Special Operations Command.

Then the color guard marched forward, and we watched as the Marine Corps flag known as the unit colors—with the official name, MCSOCOM Detachment One, embroidered in scarlet thread on a banner under the Eagle, Globe, and Anchor—was furled and cased. A four-piece band played a John Phillips Sousa song, a few generals made speeches, and then we were dismissed.

Team 4, Detachment One. (Several faces have been obscured for security.)

The Det no longer existed.

We milled around, unsure of what to do. It hadn't really sunk in. For three years these temporary buildings had been home. They housed more than a unit; it was an idea, a moment pregnant with possibility.

Some guys made plans to go out drinking, others wandered off with families. I shook a few hands, found Tracy and the kids, and headed to the airport to drop off her and Kallie. They would fly to North Carolina to prepare for the closing on our new home, while Garrett and I drove across the country.

After leaving them at the airport, he and I returned to the cottage we had rented on Del Mar Beach, just across the boat basin from the Det-One compound. While Garrett slept, I reflected on the countless dives I had performed in the boat basin, and the hundreds of hydrographic surveys and small-boat landings I conducted along this coast. I was excited to head into a new challenge and felt that the school was the right place for me. I loaded the car with the remainder of our belongings; a moving truck would arrive with our shipment in a week or so. I got some sleep and woke early, rousing Garrett and loading the final items in the car. He slept in the backseat, and I pointed the car toward the rising sun in the east.

CHAPTER 17
FORMING MARSOC

I reveled in longships with oars; I loved polished
lances, arrows in the skirmish, the shapes of
doom that others shake to see. Carnage suited
me; heaven put those things in me somehow.
—Homer, *The Odyssey*

After four days of driving—with stops to play in a freak snowstorm in California; eat dinner at Big Nose Kate's Saloon in Tombstone, Arizona; see how fast we could drive on the long, flat stretches of landscape of North Texas, punctuated only by oil derricks; and after taking a circuitous route through the Southeast to hit as many states as possible—Garrett and I made it to Jacksonville, North Carolina after sunset on the fourth day. We met up with Tracy and Kallie in a hotel room in town for a dinner of mediocre hamburgers.

Tracy had already signed the mountains of paperwork at the closing, so by the time Garrett and I arrived, we were homeowners. Since our shipment of household goods wasn't due to arrive for a few days, I used the time to paint. Tracy had already decided on the colors, a separate one for nearly every room. On blank white walls, she taped color swatches. I headed to the local home-improvement store and returned with gallons of paint and supplies, and she kept the kids busy exploring the town of Jacksonville.

Jacksonville hadn't changed much since I was last there for Infantry Training School in 1987. The primary establishments catered to the needs of young Marines. The streets housed rows of bars, tattoo parlors, laundromats, and barbershops, with the occasional pawn shop thrown in for when you needed money for one of the other establishments. In the intervening years, they had added a few more restaurants, upgraded the local mall slightly, and renovated the town's movie theater. So, while Tracy and the kids watched movies, I slapped twelve different colors of paint on over 2500 square feet of walls in just a few days, after which I made the solemn vow (to which I have largely held) never to paint again.

I had taken several weeks of leave in conjunction with the move, but after a few days, I was eager to find out where I would be working and to meet the Marines. I drove across the base to a portion of the camp called Stone Bay, where eventually the MARSOC compound would be. At present, the primary inhabitants were at the Marine Corps rifle range. Regardless of job, age, or duty, each Marine spends a minimum of one week per year on the range to qualify with their primary weapon, either the service rifle or pistol, or in many cases, both.

In a tiny, fenced-in compound in the corner of the camp was the home of the Special Operations Training Group, and within that compound were two buildings dedicated to the Special Missions Branch. This was the seed corn that would be used to build the Marine Special Operations School.

I parked and wandered into several wrong buildings before I was directed to the two concrete-slab structures at the far end of the compound. Across an open field ringed by high chain-link stood two shoot houses, and in the field a group of Marines organized themselves for a training run. I stopped and watched as the breach team moved toward the entry point, weapons covering doors and windows. The breacher fumbled a bit with the charge before running the explosive Nonel back to his firing position. I noted instructors observing and taking notes that would be covered in the debrief. The instructor checked the charge placement and the location of all Marines before giving the breacher the thumbs-up. Though I couldn't hear, I saw him touch the push-to-talk button and knew he was whispering into his throat mic, "The breach is set."

I've heard the calls so many times I knew the transmissions and their cadence by heart.

"I have control, I have control, I have control. Stand by: five… four…three…" The number two was replaced by the crack of a sniper shot eliminating a roving sentry. I pressed my fingers into my ears as the call of "one" was overshadowed by the low thump of a water charge buckling the steel door.

I didn't want to interrupt their training, so I headed for the office door. As the shooters flooded through the breach point, one of the instructors noticed me. A giant dressed in a tan Nomex fire-retardant flight suit turned and jogged toward me.

"Can I help you?"

"Yeah, I'm Master Sergeant Dailey. I'm checking in."

His massive face broke into a grin, "Oh hey. We knew you were coming, but weren't expecting you for a week or so. I'm Eden Pearl."

"Yeah, I'm not really here. I just wanted to get the lay of the land and meet anyone who was around. I don't want to keep you if you are busy."

"No, let's head in the office. Most of us are out at the shoot house, but there are a few guys around."

The Special Missions Branch was split into two main sections: CQB, which also contained the breacher section, and R&S, which contained the snipers.

The office space was long and narrow, filled with two rows of dented, navy-gray desks stacked with papers and books. Random objects sat beside desks—bicycles, dumbbells, and old, wooded ammunition crates filled with God knows what. The walls were plastered with pinups and our shoot house targets. A whiteboard in the corner contained a list of the stupidest comments made by students, things like: "I shoot pretty good until I actually start shooting," or, "It's just not hitting where I'm aiming!"

Stenciled on the wall were the four sacrosanct commandments of the religion of the range.

1. Treat every weapon as if it were loaded, even after you have ensured it to be unloaded.
2. Never let your muzzle cover anything you are not willing to destroy.
3. Keep your finger straight, off the trigger, and outside of the trigger guard until you are up on target with the intention to shoot.
4. Be sure of your target and consider its foreground and background.

Eden ran off to his desk and came back with a tan ball cap. The front was embroidered with the Special Missions Training Branch logo. He handed it to me. I turned it around. Across the back, in small block letters, my nickname "Ranger" was embroidered. The recon community is small. Nicknames and reputations precede you.

The back of Eden's cap read "Mosh Pit." He was a fun-loving time bomb, the sort of guy that worked hard and played harder. But he was an absolute professional at work. His knowledge and work ethic and passion for teaching impressed me. As soon as I had the opportunity, I made him the lead CQB instructor.

Several years later, on August 16, 2009, while returning from conducting a raid in the Afghan province of Herat, Eden's vehicle hit an IED. Eden was burned over 95 percent of his body. The doctors credited his incredible musculature with keeping him alive, although he was very seriously wounded. Eden held onto life for six years, supported by his wife Alisha and their daughter. I was honored to be able to attend his retirement ceremony in their home in San Antonio, near the Brook Army Medical Center where he was receiving treatment. Master Sergeant Eden Pearl finally succumbed to his injuries on December 20, 2015.

***

Several weeks later when I officially checked in, I met the branch's officer in charge. He shook my hand and said, "Welcome, Ranger! I look forward to working with you. There's someone that wants to meet you at the MARSOC headquarters. Can you take a drive with me?"

"Do we need to do it now, or can it wait until I get settled in?"

"No, he wanted me to bring you right over."

"OK, let's go."

The drive from the Stone Bay compound to the temporary offices being used by MARSOC took nearly thirty minutes. It was a drive I would get used to making—often several times a day as we began to grow.

As he drove, we chatted about training and other odds and ends, but he seemed reluctant to explain why I was being summoned. I didn't know many of the MARSOC component staff.

We found a parking space on the backside of the building known as "H-1," a massive, three-story brick structure that also housed the Second Marine Expeditionary Force Headquarters. He escorted me to the office of a senior officer in the headquarters, knocked on the open door, and walked in. I followed. When the colonel stood, I stepped forward and stuck my arm out, prepared to shake hands. Instead, he picked up a newspaper and slapped it down on the desk in front of me.

Calling it a newspaper might be giving too much credence to the *Marine Corps Times*. It is like our version of *The Enquirer*, usually filled with sensationalistic rumor and speculation, without a great deal of reliance on fact. I have been unable to locate the issue, but the cover read something like, "Disgruntled Det-One."

Before he even introduced himself, he glared over his desk at me. "Are you disgruntled?"

"I wasn't when I walked in here."

"What the fuck does that mean?" I can't recall much else, except that the conversation went downhill after that. Sometime later the colonel and I started over, and we now get along swimmingly.

There was a good bit of resentment that went both ways. I can't speak for anyone else, but for my part I felt that Colonel Coates and Lieutenant Colonel Kozeniesky, and the members of the Det-One staff, should have been offered key leadership positions in MARSOC. Because the Det had consisted primarily of West Coast Recon Marines, there were hurt feelings in some East Coast Marines who felt they should have been invited. Ultimately, it was going to be impossible to assuage feelings retroactively, so the best way forward was simply to get to work.

Mike checked in shortly after me, and we quickly got to work going over the lessons we had learned and covering the changes that I wanted to make with the cadre. In a training institution, there is a tendency to default to teaching techniques and using SOPs that make conducting the training easier and safer. This doesn't always serve the purpose of best preparing Marines for combat. So, we critically examined each course and lesson plan looking for ways to improve. I also impressed on the instructors the imperative to ask "Why?" when there was something they didn't understand. I also covered my policy that "because it's the way we have always done it" is never an acceptable answer from anyone, myself included.

With the CQB section in solid hands, I pulled Mike aside and offered him his choice of jobs. I expected him to pick the sniper section, but he didn't hesitate. "I want to run the breacher section."

"You've got it. Just let me know what you need."

Mike was as equally gifted with explosives as he was with long-range shooting, but that still left me needing a lead sniper instructor. Fortunately, a few days later a young-looking staff sergeant walked up to my desk and handed me his service record book.

"I'm Jon Gifford, checking in to the CQB section."

"Welcome aboard. Grab a seat. Gifford, you're a sniper, right?"

"Yes, but I was promised I was coming to be a CQB instructor."

"Who promised you that?"

"That's what I was told when I got orders here."

"Well, welcome to the Marine Corps. I need a guy to run the sniper section, and you come highly regarded. I need you to take charge of the section, and we're making some changes."

"What kind of changes?"

"Have you ever seen a scope with the Horus reticle?" I asked.

"No, what is it?"

I reached over to my desk and pulled out a scope with the reticle, and a PalmPilot PDA that ran the ballistic software. I handed them across the desk to him. "Take these, get the scope on a gun, and Mike and I will show you how to use it."

In the weeks that followed, Mike and I went to the range with Jon and the rest of his cadre. We talked through some of the things we had experienced and wanted to make sure were taught. Moving in small teams through urban areas, facing a trained sniper threat, the use of periscopes, and establishing dummy sniper positions. We brought Todd Hodnett out to further refine the section's skills, and before long they were up and running.

A year later I reminded Jon of how badly he had wanted to be in the CQB section and offered him the shot to move. Predictably he replied, "Hell no, you can't move me now."

On July 29, 2012, as the chief of a Marine Special Operations Team, Gunnery Sergeant Jonathan Gifford was mortally wounded while leading an assault on an insurgent stronghold near the town of Bala Bokan in the Badghis province of Afghanistan. For his actions he was posthumously awarded the Navy Cross, the nation's second-highest honor. The MARSOF Advanced Sniper Course that Jon built is today recognized as a premier sniper course in the special-operations world. And in 2016, the headquarters of the Marine Raider Training Center was renamed Gifford Hall. A larger-than-life bronze sculpture of Giff stands watch by the front doors, and each morning and evening hundreds of students do pushups in his shadow.

**

With the courses we were currently teaching in good hands, I turned my attention to the next challenge—building special operators. When MARSOC was formed, two-thirds of the unit was derived from First and Second Force Reconnaissance companies. These units were simply disbanded and redesignated as First and Second Marine Special Operations Battalions. The remaining third of the organization was created from a unit the Marines Corps had recently formed, the Foreign

Military Training Unit, later renamed the Marine Special Operations Advisor Group (MSOAG). This unit had been formed (at least partially) in a bid to forestall the creation of MARSOC. The Marine Corps' rationale, as I understand it, was that if they designated a unit to focus on foreign internal defense—a mission that had long been the bread and butter of the Army Special Forces—the Marines Corps could demonstrate commitment to working *with* USSOCOM without actually providing forces *to* USSOCOM, thereby sating the SecDef's appetite. But it was not to be. Ultimately, First and Second Force Recon Companies, First and Second Special Missions Training Branches, and the newly redesignated MSOAG were transferred to form MARSOC.

When it was formed, MSOAG developed its own training program, requesting help from us only when they needed specific skills. The Force Recon Marines arrived with a high level of training, but if we hoped to be recognized as a serious special-operations force, we needed a training program that would produce a consistent product: an operator capable of executing the SOCOM tasks that we had been assigned. I started working on laying out the framework of the training program we would need to create.

Unfortunately, there were some in the MARSOC headquarters with zero special-operations experience, who felt that any Marine should be able to execute any task they were given. These staff members questioned the need for a lengthy and expensive training course.

Often, the best way to win a long war is through insurgency. Bide your time, operate behind the scenes, look for opportunities to get your ideas in front of others, and don't worry if you don't get credit for it. So, we worked to build a concept that we initially dubbed the Operator Training Course (this was later changed to the Individual Training Course, or ITC). I printed reams of PowerPoint briefs outlining the course, learning outcomes, training requirements, and necessary logistical support. Then, frequently early in the morning as I drove to work, I would stop by H-1 and distribute them on desks, slide them under doors, or leave them in the output trays of printers in the MARSOC area.

I began hearing references to the course come up in conversation. It was mentioned during meetings. At every opportunity, those of us in the SMTB (now the Marine Raider Training Center) evangelized, working to make others see the need for the course. Soon we began fielding questions about budgeting, materials, and manpower. Finally, in early 2007, as I sat in a chair wedged against the wall in a packed conference room attending a meeting, the MARSOC commander, Major General Helijk, blurted out, "When am I going to get a brief on this ITC? I need to know more about it."

"Sir"—I stood up and pushed myself through the gathered mass so that he could see who was speaking—"let me get a time scheduled with your staff. We'd love to bring you up to speed."

CHAPTER 18
MAKING RAIDERS

*My title is Marine Raider. I will never
forget the tremendous legacy and sacrifice
of those who came before me.*
—First stanza of the Raider Creed

esigning a course to train special operators isn't rocket science. I had the good fortune to be able to examine what Special Forces, SEALs, and foreign special-ops units were doing, and of course we borrowed as liberally as possible from Marine reconnaissance training. My goal was to pay attention to their lessons learned, and to avoid as many mistakes as possible while capitalizing on everyone else's successes. That part was fun and easy. The challenging part was managing what the military calls D.O.T.M.L.P.F. considerations, or: doctrine, organization, training, materiel, leadership, and education, personnel, and facilities. Doing that for a nine-plus month course that was set to begin in less than six months was aptly described as trying to build an aircraft while in flight.

We made a list of the things we wanted to teach and tried to lay them out in a sensible format, starting with basics and working up. In the early days, we were only accepting Marines with an infantry background. But we couldn't rely on that happening forever, so we first had to understand the basic level of training every Marine receives, consider that as our "target population description," then build from there. You need a firm grounding in infantry skills before you can learn reconnaissance skills. You must crawl before you walk, and walk before you run.

Initially, the idea was to break each class into team-sized units and have a couple of instructors serve as the team leadership, with total responsibility for their training. I wanted to focus as much on experiential learning as possible, spending weeks in the field teaching by doing, learning through repetition, with each iteration growing in scope and complexity.

Unfortunately, because our instructors were sourced from several units, not everyone had the same level of skills, so we were compelled to take a more conventional approach to training. In many cases, one instructor used PowerPoint slides to teach a class before heading out to rehearse and learn. It wasn't optimal, but it worked.

While I was busy with ITC, other Marines had been assigned to develop and implement the MARSOC Assessment and Selection Program. Prospective candidates who met the basic physical fitness and intelligence requirements underwent a several-week assessment whose contents are still closely guarded, but which consists of psychological and physical testing designed to measure candidates against the ten MARSOC attributes:

> *Adaptability*—The ability to continuously evaluate information about the present situation and change your plan or actions as the situation changes.

> *Dependability*—A dependable person can be counted on to reliably get things done as they should, when they should, with little or no supervision.

> *Determination*—Sustaining a high level of effort over long periods despite the situation becoming difficult, stressful, frustrating, and/or boring.

> *Effective Intelligence*—The ability to solve practical problems when a book solution is not available.

Initiative—The internal drive to take charge and get the job done without being told that something needs to be accomplished. Individuals with initiative are self-starters and act in the absence of authority, supervision, or orders.

Interpersonal Skills—The ability to interact and possibly influence various other personalities with a minimum of unnecessary strife or friction.

Integrity—The ability to do the right thing when nobody else is watching or the chances of being caught are remote.

Physical Ability—Having the necessary physical attributes and functional fitness required to do one's job.

Stress Tolerance—The ability to deal with ambiguous, dangerous, high-pressure, and/or frustrating events while keeping in control of emotions/actions and maintaining composure and effectiveness.

Teamwork—Working well within a team or group. Being able to work in a large or small group to finish a task regardless of one's relationship with those individuals.

The physical testing ensures that candidates have strong backs and hard feet. The psychological testing ensures that they possess the mental agility and stability to be successful in challenging and austere special-operations environments.

Assessment and Selection places these Marines in situations that provide opportunities to demonstrate whether they possess, or do not possess, the above attributes in sufficient quantities—understanding that some of these attributes are more stable than others, while some can be developed through training. After the assessment, a selection board made up of seasoned MARSOC operators evaluates each candidate's performance, balanced against the recommendations of the psychological staff. Those who are selected receive orders to attend the next ITC. The first course was scheduled to begin in September 2008.

***

On May 5, 2008, in a small ceremony on an open field beside the obstacle course, I retired from the Marine Corps after more than twenty-one years of service. I was honored that quite a few Marines and former Marines, friends, and brothers whose careers touched mine at some point showed up to see me off. Following the ceremony, we proceeded to my house for the traditional post-retirement party, lubricated by kegs of beer. The highlight, as always, was the presentation of the paddle.

There is a tradition in Recon that has carried over to MARSOC. When a Marine leaves the unit, if they were respected, they are presented a paddle. The symbol of our amphibious heritage. The handle of the paddle is wrapped in fancy work, using parachute cord of various colors, each with a special significance. The wood is sanded smooth and stained or painted. The blade of the paddle is decorated with testaments to the recipient's service, military awards, and badges, or other items designating qualifications. An engraved plaque is attached which lists the dates of "Insert" (joined the unit) and "Extract" (left the unit), along with a memorable quote or two.

The legend holds that this tradition was instituted by the Raiders of WWII, who upon arriving at the unit were issued a paddle that they were responsible for keeping throughout their tour. As the tour was drawing to a close, the paddle would be "stolen" and decorated by members of the unit, to be presented to them before their departure. This has become one of Recon's fondest traditions.

Unfortunately, having spoken with many WWII Raiders, this is another example of the truth being less important than the legend. It stands to reason that the WWII Raiders had more pressing topics of concern than lugging a five-foot wooden paddle through the jungles of the Pacific island-hopping campaign, much less the arts-and-crafts supplies necessary to prepare and adorn the paddle. When I asked a Raider who went by the name of Mudhole, a man who took small boats ashore to the island of Makin, how he marked his paddle, he looked at me as if I had been kicked in the head. "We just left them in the boats and grabbed one when it was time to go. Why would I need a special paddle?" Additionally, most Raiders only left the unit after being wounded, so there was no time to prepare and present a paddle to someone who was departing.

Recently, some research seems to pinpoint that the tradition began in the post-Vietnam era, when a recon boathouse received a new shipment of paddles. The Marine in charge of the boat house decided to hold onto the old paddles to use as gifts. This tradition has grown over the years, and paddles have increased in length and complexity, intricately carved on CNC machines from exotic woods, to the point that they would be impractical and inefficient for propelling a small craft through a crashing surf zone. But they are among the most highly prized possessions of any Recon Marine or Raider.

The beauty of the tradition is that, as with many things, its empirical truth is far less important than its meaning. The paddle's power is as a symbol that originated in the days before outboard motors were common. Each man on a boat team is responsible for pulling their own weight. If they don't paddle in unison, the craft can't maintain its azimuth. So, on one hand, the paddle is a symbol of teamwork necessary in small teams doing dangerous work. On the other hand, the boat is controlled by the coxswain, the leader and most experienced member of the boat team. The coxswain uses his paddle to help steer the boat, so the paddle is also a symbol of leadership.

I have heard many former Recon Marines explain the SOP in their house. If the house catches fire, paddles take precedence over children, because children have legs. Joking yes, but barely; the paddle is a symbol of love from a group that doesn't use words like love easily.

Retiring from active duty should have felt stranger than it did, but I had already been hired to return as a civilian to serve as the deputy director of the Special Operations Training Branch. I would be doing essentially the same job, and there was too much to do for me to spend too long reminiscing. And other than not needing to shave every day, not much changed. I still wore a uniform, but now it consisted of polo shirts and khakis rather than Marine Corps camouflage.

Now, I encourage any Marine leaving the service to take some time to mark the occasion, whether it is after four-year enlistment or a thirty-year career. A post-military gap year, if you will. Even if it is far less than a year. I think it would be ideal to do something significant to mark the occasion and provide time to reflect on what the years of service meant, but also to focus on leaving the warrior mantle behind and returning to being a citizen. Ideally, I would have loved to set out on a hike of the Appalachian Trail, but with family responsibilities and looming deadlines for starting ITC, I took little more than a long weekend before heading back to the office.

Lieutenant Colonel "Buster" Crabb had been assigned as my boss, and together we pushed the handful of instructors and staff that we had to prepare for the upcoming course. We attacked the mountain of work required, from developing the curriculum, to typing lesson plans and student handouts, ordering equipment, and finding a place for a class of sixty students to live. We pressed nearly condemned WWII buildings back into service as barracks, and had temporary trailers brought in and configured as office spaces, classrooms, and bathroom-and-shower facilities. And just like at Det-One, soon FedEx and DHL trucks were lining up to drop off equipment: rucksacks and ballistic vests piled among water cans, stretchers, and medical gear. The armory was overflowing with weapons and optics. For physical training, we purchased barbells, plates, kettlebells, and weight sleds, and stored them in shipping containers beside the large open field across the street from the barracks, next to the obstacle course. Another container stored boxing gloves, strike pads, focus mitts, headgear, and rubber pistols and knives for combatives training.

We plotted routes through the woods for running. Instructors worked on rehabilitating an old trail network that ran through the woods behind the barracks. We developed routes that meandered in and out of streams, and staged ammunition cans full of dirt for weight to be used for farmer's carries.

Since the nearest swimming pool was nearly an hour roundtrip, we marked off an area with buoys in the New River that borders the camp, until our pool was built. The only requirement was that while students were in the water, we had to keep one Marine on alligator watch. It was doubtful that an alligator would attack a swimmer in such a large group, but it was better to be safe than sorry. Often the wedge-shaped head could be seen watching from a safe distance, and at night the two red dots of their eyes reflected as Marines on watch panned their flashlights back and forth.

And so, with our growing cadre, we began to solidify the training schedule. We built and rehearsed classes, labored over training material, and crafted field exercises to provide training opportunities just outside of the students' reach, to force growth. We rehearsed presentations and murder-boarded each other. A murder board consists of a group of instructors play-acting as students receiving a class, peppering the instructor with questions. Then, when the class is over, we tear apart the instruction. What could be better? Where did the students lose interest? How could we improve learning and retention?

I advocated, and still do, the use of personal stories wherever possible, to provide examples and turn what could be a boring class into an interactive learning experience. As an instructor, it's natural to want your students to think that you are infallible, but having the courage to tell them about a situation where you struggled will make a much greater impression and stick with them much longer than "no shit, there I was" stories.

Starting a new unit of over two thousand Marines meant that we had to start somewhere. Training for the first Marine Special Operations Teams to deploy consisted of little more than the standard Force Recon pre-deployment training program. And obviously, our initial ITC instructor cadre had to teach a course that they themselves had not attended. The requirement, however, was that each instructor complete Assessment and Selection. Those that were not selected left the unit. Those that made it went to work preparing for the first ITC class, keeping the five Special Operations Truths in mind:

I. Humans are more important than hardware.
II. Special operations forces (SOF) cannot be mass-produced.
III. Quality is better than quantity.
IV. Competent SOF cannot be created after emergencies occur. (Of course, that is what we had been tasked with doing, so we focused on the first three.)
V. Most special operations require non-SOF support.

The first ITC class was scheduled for September 2008. Many of the students were already in MARSOC, some had already deployed with teams, and most of the others were Recon Marines. There were a few from MSOAG, but all were infantry Marines, meaning they had a working knowledge of the basics. Soon, we began opening A&S to male Marines from any specialty, and pilots, trumpet players, admin clerks, and weathermen would take up the challenge and make it to ITC. But the foundational training we established in 2008 has allowed the instructors to build these Marines into Raiders.

In 2016, A&S was opened to women; but to date, while a handful have attended, none have successfully been selected for training in ITC.

I continued with my exploration of how we learn, and researched ways to improve the way we taught and the instructional techniques we used. Buster and I studied learning theory and advanced instructional techniques, and fortunately he agreed with me that it was as much our responsibility to build character and develop an organizational culture as it was to teach hard skills. We borrowed a page from the commander of the Second Raider Battalion in WWII, Lieutenant Colonel Evans Carlson, and held regular Gung-Ho meetings among the instructors, in which everyone's voice carried equal weight, and every suggestion or comment was given consideration. With the ITC class, we looked for opportunities to discuss the role the MARSOC attributes played in mission success or failure. Rather than build Marines who could just "do things," we needed Marines who could walk into a complex situation in an austere environment—often working with a partner force and/ or government and civilian agencies—quickly learn to recognize and understand the competing equities, then evaluate options and make the tough decisions needed to accomplish their mission. Ultimately, we were building tough men who could solve complex problems.

To that end, I wanted to focus heavily on observation. One of the most valuable skills in problem-solving is simply to be aware of your surroundings. At the most basic level, this can help identify booby traps or collect information on the enemy. In the shoot house, you cannot shoot faster than you can see and identify; and when conducting meetings with partner-nation personnel or sources, the ability to observe and take note of actions and reactions, and pick up on body language and awkward glances, can mean the difference between mission accomplishment or death.

The main technique we employed is an exercise common to snipers, called Kim's Game. The title is derived from the Rudyard Kipling story *Kim*, in which the title character, a poor Indian boy from the streets of Lahore, learns that he is really the son of a now-deceased British color sergeant. Because he was raised as an Indian, he can blend into the environment seamlessly. When his true identity is discovered, he is trained by the British for espionage. One of the techniques used to heighten his observation and memory skills was called "the jewel game." In the game, Kim would be shown a group of jewels for a limited time. He was then expected to describe them in exacting detail. We used variations on this theme, beginning with the students gathered around a poncho that would be pulled away to reveal items they were expected to memorize. As their proficiency increased, we created distractions or hid items along a run route, or camouflaged items and placed them at the opposite end of a field, or flashed a PowerPoint slide with an image of a passport in between slides in a presentation. The students were never sure what they would be asked to recall, and so they began to take in everything.

One of the biggest challenges that Buster and I faced was convincing the instructors of our unconventional training methodologies. They were all seasoned combat veterans who had been successful in doing things one way. Now we were asking them to trust in methodologies that were often foreign, and at times bizarre. In what would prove to be my worst misuse of government funds, I purchased one hundred licenses for speed-reading software that I believed would sharpen the senses and increase observational speed and the ability to rapidly pick up and identify targets. I still think it might have worked, but I couldn't get the instructors behind it.

I also attempted to work on the mental aspect by instituting meditation practice. I brought in a meditation instructor who kindly volunteered her time. This was my first foray into guided meditation, although I have continued to practice it over the years and find it incredibly beneficial. Although I could see that many of the instructors were skeptical, they sat and gave her their undivided attention as she explained the benefits of mindfulness practice and described the meditation session we were going to perform. Following her brief lecture, she requested that we all sit and participate in a closed-eye meditation. She placed a rhythmic compact disc in the player, and we began. Once or twice as I sat focusing on my breath, I heard the door at the far end of the classroom open and close, but each time returned to focusing on my breath. At the end of the session, I opened my eyes to discover her and me alone in the classroom; everyone else had slipped out the back door. You win some, you lose some.

We brought in outside professionals from various disciplines, both to allow our instructors to learn from them, and to see how they taught and hopefully pick up a few traits that might be useful. Instructors like Paul Howe, Todd Hodnett, Sensi James Williams, Kyle Lamb, Todd Jarrett, and others. Every guest instructor provided some nugget of information to learn from, and each demonstrated a successful but wildly unique teaching method. I have come to believe that being a successful teacher is simply a product of having a huge toolbox full of tools and knowing when and how to use each one. Being a great teacher comes from truly caring about the success of your students, and a willingness to meet them where they are and to employ every tool in the toolbox, if needed, to get them to learn.

We knew the students graduating from ITC would be deploying to Afghanistan soon after graduation, so each instructor used every trick in the book to cram as much capability into them in the time we had.

The final (and most important) ingredient in a successful special operator goes by many names. We capture it as "mental toughness" in the MARSOC attributes, and it has been called the X-factor, or the "special sauce." Dr. Angela Duckworth has famously written about it as "grit." It exists at the intersection of passion and perseverance. She defines it as "a goal you care about so much that it organizes and gives meaning to almost everything you do."

I am convinced that grit is like a muscle—it can be built and strengthened through adversity. The trick is in keeping the challenge in the sweet spot: achievable, but tough. Realistic, but robust. You get hard by doing hard things, and the one principle of warfare that is not likely to change is that it will require hard motherfuckers.

One of the challenges in special operations training is that we don't want people who don't want to be there. It is a voluntary organization. We hate quitters. I think one reason is that we all, from time to time, are near the breaking point. We don't want the thought of quitting brought to the forefront of our minds, where it could latch on and slowly spread like cancer. Quitters are ostracized, so it is best to remove them from the team as quickly as possible. I hate to see someone quit because I know that they will carry that failure for the rest of their life.

I have found that one of the best ways to make Marines think long and hard before quitting is to make them recognize that by quitting, they are increasing the burden on the rest of their team. If a student quits in the field, the equipment from their ruck will have to be redistributed. Each man's load will grow. To help drive home this point, we brought back an old recon tradition, the rope. The idea of carrying ropes goes back to Carlson's Raiders. Each man was required to carry a "toggle rope." This twelve-to-fifteen-foot piece of rope had an eyelet woven into one end and a wooden toggle affixed to the other. This allowed the ropes to be connected to scale obstacles, or create rope bridges to traverse chasms. The idea is that each rope provided capability to the team. Each length of rope added to the height of the obstacle that could be surmounted.

We award each student a sling rope, which is tied in a loop and worn during all training. This serves the functional purposes of both readily identifying students, as well as providing the capability to quickly create a Swiss seat for rappelling. Having the rope on hand also allows us to fill any extra free time practicing mandatory knots. But the larger reason was to serve as a constant reminder of the burden of shared responsibility. When a student decides to quit, they need only remove their rope and turn it in to an instructor. But the act of surrendering the rope has caused many to rethink and recommit themselves to persevering.

By the time the sixty Marines arrived for the inaugural ITC class in September 2008, we were ready. Mike and I tried to instill the lessons we had learned at the Det. Movement under heavy load is the best measure of fitness and builder of grit. The ten-mile ruck movement became the standard measure of fitness. A ruck with forty-five pounds of dry weight plus enough water to remain hydrated. And the pre-ruck instructions served as a guide to success in training and in life: Don't be light, don't be late, don't be last.

As this book is preparing to go to publication, ITC Class 32 will soongraduate. My title has now changed to Training and Education Branch Director, and I don't get to be nearly as involved in the training as I would like to be, but I am not needed. The course has grown and improved, and the instructors and the instruction are light-years beyond where we were, and what it was in the beginning. Our continued success falls on the shoulders of each instructor who strives to make each class better than the one before it. It is a pleasure to watch and an honor to be a part of.

CHAPTER 19

THOUGHTS ON TWENTY YEARS OF WAR

Now that their long war was over, they could
get on with the proper concern of all civilized
nations, which is to prepare for the next one.
—Terry Pratchett

So now we come to the end of this memoir, a lifetime in the making and more than a year in the writing.

In *Quartered Safe Out Here*, George McDonald Frasier wrote of his time as a member of the British Fourteenth, fighting the Japanese in Burma. "Looking back over fifty-odd years, life is like a piece of string with knots in it. The knots being those moments that live in the mind forever, and the intervals being hazy, half-recalled times when I have a fair idea what was happening in a general way but cannot be sure of dates or places or even the exact order in which events took place." This is as accurate a description as one can hope for of the way the mind works—choosing specific events to recall in stark relief, while others fade and commingle.

I've tried my best to describe the "knot" moments in a way that does them justice, and to fill in the "hazy" times—those memories worn smooth, like stones tumbled for decades in the stream of my subconscious—through focused recollection and the support of friends who were there. Any errors of omission or commission rest solely on my shoulders.

In 2022, by a fortuitous twist of fate, as I was writing this book, I had the opportunity to schedule a reunion of many of my Det-One brothers. MARSOC was hosting a "Raider Week" to honor our fallen, stop to capture our present, and focus forward to the anticipated challenges of an uncertain future. I felt that this would be as good an opportunity to gather as there ever would be, and so with the support of the unit, I reached out to the Marines I was in contact with and found the response was overwhelming. Many of us had not seen each other since the day the Det-One unit flag was folded in 2006, and the occasion would come close to marking the nineteenth anniversary of our activation.

I set about the work of tracking everyone down. Through an endless series of emails, text chains, phone calls, and social-media pleas, I was able to invite most of the Marines and sailors of the Det. They were spread far and wide, across the United States, South America, Africa, the Middle East, Europe and Ukraine.

Master Sergeant Michael Glauner had lost his battle with cancer and attended only in memory. Everyone else seemed to have done well for themselves. Among us, there were doctors, MBAs, park rangers, business owners, and C-suite executives. Some, like me, continued to work for the Marine Corps in some capacity, and many worked for three-letter agencies. This, plus the fact that we generally went by first names, explains my using first names here for the enlisted members of the unit. I've referred to the officers by rank and name because there is still a large part of me that is a Marine, and that is what we do.

A few of our members still serve on active duty. Colonel Coates, in retirement, continues to contribute as a mentor to MEU commanders. In 2016 he was inducted into the USSOCOM Commando Hall of Honor.

I arrived early at the hotel conference room we had reserved as our base of operations, and filled coolers with beer and lined the shelves with bottles of booze. I was excited to see my old teammates and friends, but nervous, too. I didn't know what to expect, or how they would feel about the way I had tried to keep our legacy alive in the hearts and minds of today's Raiders.

Slowly they began trickling in. They were easily recognizable by their stride, their laugh, or the turn of their head; but the Marines with whom I served had all been replaced with older, grayer versions of the men I had known. Most were still very fit for their age, many still fit for twenty-year-olds.

But the years and gray hairs melted away in the time it took to crack a beer. Old jokes were told, old disagreements picked up, and old stories brought an avalanche of memories.

For three days we laughed and talked and drank. We drank a lot, reminisced, and I was able to confirm parts of my story and add detail and color to old recollections.

Detachment One reunion in 2022. We are gathered in the Marine Raider Training Center Heritage Hall.

As a group, we traveled to the MARSOC compound to be present for the "Raider Night" ceremony, where the members of the graduating ITC class are presented with their Marine Special Operator Insignia. We had the honor of being joined by several of our original WWII

Raider forefathers. I was humbled as the young Raiders treated both groups with the respect reserved for standard-bearers.

We toured the MARSOC compound, and I showed them the school, the shoot houses, the ranges, the dog kennel, and the long, black, granite walls that bear the names of Jon Gifford, Eden Pearl, and the other forty-six Raider fallen.

On the final night of the reunion, we took over a local bar for our festivities. But eventually they closed, and we found ourselves sitting outside in a soft rain, drinking cans of beer purchased against just such an eventuality. One of the other team leaders looked at me and said, "Hey, I know we had our differences." He went on to recall the event that he felt had caused it. I only vaguely remembered the incident. I had some completely different reason for not liking him, but now I couldn't recall what it was, and truthfully, I don't think I have remembered it for a very long time. Its very unimportance made me think of the St. Crispin's Day speech from Shakespeare's *Henry the Fifth*:

> *Old men forget: yet all shall be forgot,*
> *But he'll remember, with advantages,*
> *What feats he did that day...*
> *...We few, we happy few, we band of brothers;*
> *For he to-day that sheds his blood with me*
> *Shall be my brother; be he ne'er so vile,*
> *This day shall gentle his condition...*

***

I recently came in to work to find a small award folder on my desk. Inside was a certificate and a tiny box holding a little bronze lapel pin. On the face of the pin is the seal of the United States, and beneath it the number 35, indicating my total years of military and government service. It's shocking, daunting actually, how quickly time goes. I walk the halls of the Raider Training Center and look at seventeen years' worth of photos of commanding officers and senior enlisted leaders hanging in a long row, and remember each for his strengths and weaknesses.

While the pin was intended as a recognition, it has had the opposite effect. Each time I rub it between my fingers I begin to get claustrophobic. I have a vision of myself sitting at this same desk, rubbing other pins bearing the numerals 40, 45, 50...I swear I won't grow old and die here, but don't know how to stop it.

There is an axiom as old as it is true. No matter how indispensable you believe you are, the day after you depart, the Marine Corps will still be there. I love the Marines—being around them and talking to them. I love sitting in the back of a classroom and listening to an instructor teach. I love standing in front of students and sharing stories with them. I once stayed at my job because I felt they needed me. Later I realized the opposite is true.

Now I wonder if it is time to move on. Marines will still do their jobs, fight wars or train to, all without me. Maybe a story will be told that includes me, and when they share the stories perhaps some small part of me will live on. But soon, those hearing the stories will not know my name. It is simply the Marine Corps circle of life.

I return regularly to Marcus Aurelius. He too suffered from impostor syndrome, and I have come to accept that I will never beat mine. I continue to read and learn from the Stoics and countless other philosophers and wise men, and am finally beginning to find peace with myself. I know I could not have achieved the things I did without the constant, looming specter of fear of being found inadequate. We all shared it to some degree, and I think that it is what made us collectively so good: the fear of failure, the fear of rejection, the fear of letting the team, and the Marine Corps down. Colonel Coates built loyalty to him because he didn't seek it. He demanded loyalty to the institution, the unit, the mission. He set the example and held the standard. Our fear of failing him drove us, and we worshipped him for it.

I learned that while there are few things in my control, I always retain the ability to view rucking as meditation rather than misery, and that decision has expanded to become the way I view all of life. The tightness that gives way to aching in the calves, the pull of the pack straps, the weariness in the thighs, the salt-soaked clothing. I can't control the pain, but I can embrace it as penance for some real or imagined sin, or consider it a down payment on a well of resilience that will be drawn upon one day. Mental toughness on layaway.

I still keep a loaded ruck in my car and shoulder it several days a week. I hike trails and dirt roads in circles, to reflect as I exercise myself and exorcise my demons.

Sometimes the ghosts of brothers come along. They come out less frequently now. Usually on special days. I used to talk to them, but now we just trudge along together for a while. I have nothing to say that they don't know, and they are silent.

This writing has provided the opportunity I may not otherwise have taken for reflection. I have considered: if the opportunity were permitted me to go back in time, what advice I would give to my younger self. I have decided that this is a fool's errand. It wouldn't matter what I said to him. He wouldn't have listened. Nor should he have. What would I have told him? To eat better or drink less? Maybe some investment advice from the future would have been nice. I would probably tell him to be more present; to cherish the time with his family more. But he was invincible and could never envision how quickly time would pass. I know myself well enough to know that I wouldn't have listened to the advice of an old man, and of course, any advice that I might have taken would necessarily have changed the course of events, like a butterfly beating its wings over Africa.

The better question is, "If the younger me walked through my door today, what would he say? Would he be proud?" I hope so. I carry his excesses still, and he would doubtlessly, rightfully, tell me to lose a few pounds. But I think he would be contented, because I am.

I've had a front-row seat as history was being writ large on the page. I have been a part of making life and taking it. I've walked among giants and stood on their shoulders. We were jacks of all trades and masters of none. The past is a unique reminder of different times, some better, others worse, but they are times that shaped me; and the times I meet now, headlong, will be met remembering the creed I swore to: Never shall I forget the principles I accepted to become a Recon Marine: honor, perseverance, spirit, and heart.

I am reminded of Circe's question of Odysseus: "Must you have battle in your heart forever? The bloody toil of combat? Old contender, will you not yield to the immortal gods?"

I will not yield. It will always be there, and I will always cherish and revile it.

We each decide whether to look forward or back. To stare through the windshield, or drive while sneaking glances in the rearview mirror. This project has had me glaring fully into the rearview, and I can say that while worth it, I'm ready to turn my attention back to the here and the now, illuminated by the glow of my headlights. The future arrives all too soon.

I no longer believe in immortality. The mirror won't permit it. Nor will the cold stones that mark the resting places of friends who gave the full measure. Better men than I.

I think back to the young man in Najaf from time to time. There are some advantages to dying young, I guess. He will never live to question his worth, the difference he made, or what it was all about. He won't have to come to grips with failures as a husband and father. He will never stare into a mirror that reflects a face that is familiar but difficult to recognize. Eyes that once squinted to identify distant objects now require glasses to read a book.

Don't get me wrong. I'm glad it was him and not me. I have had a wonderful life and hope that it extends for as long as I can reasonably enjoy it. I guess I'm just becoming contemplative, a luxury of aging.

At some point, the living must reconcile with the inevitable end. Unlike him, I cannot remain a boy forever. I once thought that to admit this was to admit defeat. A mountain which, once crested, would see me hurled over the precipice of irrelevance and uselessness. And so, I fought it, but in doing so delayed my ability to recognize that from this pinnacle there is still the possibility of adventure in the distant future. And now, I can finally turn and look unencumbered to the past with clear eyes.

So, this is not my death letter, but instead an attempt to examine what that time meant to me, and how it has impacted me for good and

for ill. A chance to explain to those who have never borne witness—
without the bravado of youth, or the restraint of old age—that war is a
beautiful, horrible thing.

ACKNOWLEDGMENTS

I would double the length of this manuscript if I gave all credit to where it is due, so I will be brief and apologize to many whom I owe enormous debts.

To the men of Detachment One, thank you. It was an honor to call each of you brother. I wish I could have told all the stories that should be told and written in depth about each of you wonderful bastards.

To all those who have carried and do carry the burden and honor that comes with the titles Scout Sniper, Reconnaissance Marine, and Marine Raider. I thank you for your selfless sacrifice, and challenge you to strive each day to continue to be a worthy bearer of our extraordinary legacy.

To my parents, thank you for bringing me up surrounded by books.

To my wife, Tracy. Thank you for your continued love and support after more than thirty years of marriage. I am a lucky man, and a better man because of you.

To my children, Garrett, and Kallie, I apologize for the times when service came before family. I am proud that you have become your own people, and glad to see that if nothing else, I have given you my gift of sarcasm.

To my fellow students and the professors of the UNCW Master of Fine Arts program. You taught me how to think of myself as a writer. To Ashley Hudson, Kimi Hemingway, and Rebecca Lee, thank you for seeing something in me and cultivating it. To Nina de Gramont, thank you for teaching me how to tell a story. Clyde Edgerton, thank you for encouraging me to tell it.

Carole Avriett, thank you for believing in me when I didn't believe in myself.

To Russell Worth Parker thank you for your friendship and countless hours on the trail.

To Team 4: Sid, Mike, Bo, Eric, and Doc, thanks for always making me look good, or at least trying.

To Jon Laplume, thanks for being the highest-paid M-240 gunner in the DOD, and a great friend.

To the men of America's Team, A.T., Davey, Frankie, and Crackers. To the men of Second Platoon First Force Recon. To Willy Thom, Bill Frost, and Biker Mike for teaching me how to be a Recon Marine.

To Lieutenant Colonel John Piedmont. Your history of Detachment One served as the primary reference for my forgetful mind.

To my agent, Greg Johnson of Wordserve Literary, and to Caitlin Burdette and Alex Novak from Post Hill Press. Thank you for faith and support. Robert, thank you for your editorial patience.

Finally, to Colonel Robert J. Coates. Thank you for being an uncompromising leader and for building tough rugged bastards. From you, I learned that when the cause is just, you must be willing to burn the ships on the shore and leave no way but forward.

Never above you
Never below you
Always beside you

ABOUT THE AUTHOR

Photo by Jake Blick

John Dailey left his home in West Virginia at seventeen to join the Marines, which led to a career of over twenty years. As a Platoon Sergeant in the Marine Corps' First Force Reconnaissance Company on deployment in Australia on September 11, 2001, he and his men soon found themselves in Afghanistan battling the Taliban. In 2003 he was selected to serve as a team leader in the first Marine Corps unit assigned to US Special Operations Command—Detachment-1. Det-1's 2004 Iraq deployment solidified the Marine Corps' place in special operations and led to the formation of the Marine Special Operations Command (MARSOC). John received his MFA in creative writing from the University of North Carolina–Wilmington in 2018. John continues to train Marine Raiders and provides leadership training and performance coaching through his company, Walking Point LLC. He lives in Hubert, North Carolina, with his wife, Tracy.